AIRLINE OPERATIONS
CONTROL

This text is among the first to reveal the intricacies of an airline's Operations Control Centre; especially the thought processes, information flows, and strategies taken to mitigate disruptions.

Airline Operations Control provides a deep level of description, explanation, and detail into the activities of a range of highly professional and expert staff managing the 'sharp' end of the airline. It aims to fill a void as little is understood about this area, and very little is written for practitioners in the airline business. The book offers a comprehensive look at the make-up of the Operations Centre, its component sections, and the processes that occur both in preparing for and executing the current day's schedules. Several chapters provide real-life scenarios and demonstrate how Operations Centres manage evolving situations – what they need to take into account, and how they need to have Plan B and Plan C ready when things don't go right.

This book is designed to deliver knowledge gains to both new and experienced aviation industry practitioners with regard to vital operational aspects. Additionally, it also offers students of air transport management a readily accessible and real-world-perspective guide to a crucial function present within every airline.

Peter J. Bruce spent nearly 17 years in the airline industry, for nearly all of which he was an operations controller in an Australian domestic airline. He is recently retired from the Department of Aviation, Swinburne University of Technology in Melbourne. Peter is an FAA licensed Dispatcher.

Chris Mulholland started in aviation with Trans Australia Airlines in 1977, has held various positions in the Operations Control areas in Trans Australia Airlines, Australian Airlines, and now Qantas where he currently holds the position of Manager, Integrated Operations Centre.

MANAGING AVIATION OPERATIONS

Series Editor: Peter J. Bruce

Associate Editor: John M. C. King

The purpose of this series is to provide a comprehensive set of materials dealing with the key components of airline and airport operations. To date, this innovative approach has not been evident among aviation topics and certainly not applied to operational areas of airlines or airports. While more recent works have begun, in brief, to consider the various characteristics of operational areas, the Managing Aviation Operations series will expand coverage with far greater breadth and depth of content.

Airlines and airports are devoid of specific topic knowledge in ready-made, easy-to-read, creditable resources. Tapping into industry expertise to drive a range of key niche products will resource the industry in a way not yet seen in this domain. Therefore, the objective is to deliver a collection of specialised, internationally sourced and expertly written books to serve as readily accessible guides and references primarily for professionals within the industry. The focus of the series editors will be to ensure product quality, user readability and appeal, and transparent consistency across the range.

Airline Management Finance
The Essentials
Victor Hughes

Airline Operations Control
Peter J. Bruce and Chris Mulholland

For more information about this series, please visit:
www.routledge.com/Aviation-Fundamentals/book-series/MAO

AIRLINE OPERATIONS CONTROL

PETER J. BRUCE AND
CHRIS MULHOLLAND

LONDON AND NEW YORK

First published 2021
by Routledge
2 Park Square, Milton Park, Abingdon, Oxon OX14 4RN

and by Routledge
52 Vanderbilt Avenue, New York, NY 10017

Routledge is an imprint of the Taylor & Francis Group, an informa business

© 2021 Peter J. Bruce and Chris Mulholland

The right of Peter J. Bruce and Chris Mulholland to be identified as
authors of this work has been asserted by them in accordance with
sections 77 and 78 of the Copyright, Designs and Patents Act 1988.

All rights reserved. No part of this book may be reprinted or reproduced or utilised
in any form or by any electronic, mechanical, or other means, now known or
hereafter invented, including photocopying and recording, or in any information
storage or retrieval system, without permission in writing from the publishers.

Trademark notice: Product or corporate names may be trademarks or registered trademarks,
and are used only for identification and explanation without intent to infringe.

British Library Cataloguing-in-Publication Data
A catalogue record for this book is available from the British Library

Library of Congress Cataloging-in-Publication Data
Names: Bruce, Peter J., author. | Mulholland, Chris (Writer on aviation), author.
Title: Airline operations control / Peter J. Bruce and Chris Mulholland.
Description: Milton Park, Abingdon, Oxon; New York, NY: Routledge, 2021. |
Series: Managing aviation operations |
Includes bibliographical references and index.
Identifiers: LCCN 2020015185 (print) | LCCN 2020015186 (ebook) |
ISBN 9780815353454 (hardback) | ISBN 9780815353478 (paperback) |
ISBN 9781351136303 (ebook)
Subjects: LCSH: Airlines–Management. | Airlines–Economic aspects.
Classification: LCC HE9776 .B78 2021 (print) |
LCC HE9776 (ebook) | DDC 387.7068/5–dc23
LC record available at https://lccn.loc.gov/2020015185
LC ebook record available at https://lccn.loc.gov/2020015186

ISBN: 978-0-8153-5345-4 (hbk)
ISBN: 978-0-8153-5347-8 (pbk)
ISBN: 978-1-351-13630-3 (ebk)

Typeset in Galliard
by Newgen Publishing UK

CONTENTS

List of figures	viii
List of common abbreviations	x
Preface	xxi

PART I OPERATIONS FUNCTION	**1**
CHAPTER 1 OPERATIONS CONTROL	3
Introduction	3
Regulatory framework	4
Terminology	4
Defining the IOC	5
History	6
Location	12
Purpose and philosophy	13
Hierarchy and reporting lines	15
CHAPTER 2 COMPOSITION OF THE IOC	16
Introduction	16
IOC senior management	17
IOC staff	19
IOC duty manager	20
Operational staff	20
Operations controller	21
Flight dispatcher	38
Maintenance watch	40
Meteorology	41
Aircraft allocation/planning	41
Load control	42
Crew control	43
Commercial and customer journey management	44
ATC flow control/slot control	45

CONTENTS

Airports coordinator	45
Freight liaison	46
Social media	47
Security	47
Extended communications	48
External relationships	49
Key challenges for IOC management	50

CHAPTER 3 OPERATIONAL PLANNING AND PREPARATION	51
Introduction	51
Business factors	52
Commercial factors	55
Operational factors	58
Final IOC preparations – the handover	72

CHAPTER 4 OPERATIONAL PROCESSES	75
Introduction	75
Operational authority and autonomy	76
Systems and tools	76
Regular operations	95
Irregular operations (IROPS)	100
Operational actions and strategies	101
Potential disruptions	103
IOC response patterns (general)	104
Weather	104
Engineering	115
Air traffic	118
Crewing	120
Airport	122
Customers	124
Industrial	126
Commercial	126
Security	127
Miscellaneous	128
Worked example	128
Imminent disruptions	132

CONTENTS

PART II OPERATIONAL CONTROL IN PRACTICE   **135**
   Introduction   135

CHAPTER 5 SCENARIO-BASED INFORMATION FLOWS   137
   Introduction   137
   Brief   138
   IOC roles   138

CHAPTER 6 WEATHER SCENARIO: SNOW AT JFK AIRPORT   147
   Brief   147
   Scenario description   147
   IOC interaction   148

CHAPTER 7 WEATHER SCENARIO: THUNDERSTORMS AT SYD AIRPORT   159
   Brief   159
   Scenario description   160
   IOC interaction   160

CHAPTER 8 MULTI-ENGINEERING SCENARIO: UNSERVICEABILITIES IN THE NETWORK   175
   Brief   175
   Scenario description   175
   IOC interaction   177

CHAPTER 9 OPERATIONS CONTROL IN THE FUTURE   191
   Introduction   191
   Industry   192
   Technology   192
   Staff   193
   External influences   193
   Social media   194
   Final comment   194
   Note from the authors   195

   Bibliography   196
   Index   197

FIGURES

2.1	Internal relationships of the IOC	19
2.2	External relationships of the IOC	49
4.1	Representative Gantt chart	78
4.2	Flight blocks positioned according to IOC time zone	80
4.3	Flight blocks positioned according to UTC time zone	81
4.4	Gantt chart representing domestic or short-haul operations	83
4.5	Gantt chart representing flag or international operations	84
4.6	Information on a flight block (PUK)	85
4.7	Representation of extended maintenance work	87
4.8	Representation of maintenance icon	88
4.9	Depiction of customer connections	89
4.10	Depiction of crew connections	90
4.11	Gantt chart incorporating a timeline	91
5.1	Internal relationships in the IOC – abridged	138
5.2	Engineering contact trail	139
5.3	Pilot Crewing contact trail	141
5.4	Flight Attendant crewing contact trail	141
5.5	Customer Journey Management contact trail	142
5.6	Airport contact trail	143
5.7	Dispatch/Slot Control contact trail	144
6.1	JFK weather – status @ 1700	146
6.2	JFK weather – status @ 1740	149
6.3	JFK weather – status @ 1915	151
6.4	JFK weather – solution	156
7.1	SYD weather – status @ 1115	158
7.2	SYD weather – status @ 1120	162
7.3	SYD weather – status @ 1125	164
7.4	SYD weather – status @ 1130	168
7.5	SYD weather – solution	172
8.1	Multi-engineering – status @ 0415	174
8.2	Multi-engineering – status @ 0420	176

8.3	Multi-engineering – status @ 0515	180
8.4	Multi-engineering – status @ 0620	184
8.5	Multi-engineering – solution	188

COMMON ABBREVIATIONS

. . . .

OPERATIONAL

A/C	Aircraft
ACARS	Aircraft communication addressing and reporting system
AD	Airworthiness directive
ADF	Airline Dispatchers Federation
AFB	Air force base
AFTN	Aeronautical fixed telecommunication network
AIP	Aeronautical information publication
AIREP	Air report
AIS	Aeronautical information services
ALERFA	Alert phase
ANO	Air navigation order
ANSP	Air navigation service provider
AOC	Airline Operations Control
AOC	Air operators certificate
AOCC	Airline Operations Control Centre
AOCS	Air operations communication system
ARFF	Aviation rescue and fire fighting
ARINC	Aeronautical radio incorporated
ARMS	Aircrew resources management system
ARP	Aerodrome reference point
ASA	Air Services Australia
ASDA	Accelerate stop distance available
ASIC	Aviation security identification card
ASIR	Air safety incident report
ASIST	Aviation security incident support team

x

COMMON ABBREVIATIONS

ASM	Ad-hoc schedule message
ATA	Actual time of arrival
ATC	Air Traffic Control
ATD	Actual time of departure
ATFM	Air traffic flow management
ATIS	Automatic terminal info service
ATS	Air traffic service
ATSB	Australian Transport Safety Bureau
AVGAS	Aviation gasoline
AVTUR	Aviation turbine fuel
AZFW	Actual zero fuel weight
BOM	Bureau of Meteorology
CAA	Civil Aviation Authority
CAO	Civil aviation order
CAR	Civil aviation regulations
CASA	Civil Aviation Safety Authority
CAT	Category
CAT	Clear air turbulence
CAT I	Category I – Operations down to 200 ft, decision height and RVR above 2600 ft
CAT II	Category II – Operations down to 100 ft, decision height and RVR above 1200 ft
CAT III	Category III – No decision height and RVR above 700 ft
CBT	Computer-based training
CCRF	Cabin crew rest facility
CDAs	Continuous descent approaches
CFL	Cleared flight level
CFM	Engine manufacturer (General Electric/Safran joint company)
CG	Centre of gravity
CI	Cost index
CIP	Commercially important person
CIQ	Customs, immigration & quarantine
CJM	Customer journey manager/management
COBT	Calculated off-blocks time
COCO	Catering coordinator
COSE	Centre of service excellence
CRM	Crew resource management
CSM	Customer service manager/management
CTMS	Central traffic management system

COMMON ABBREVIATIONS

DA	Decision altitude
DARP	Dynamic airborne route planning
DETRESFA	Distress phase
DH	Decision height
DME	Distance measuring equipment
DOT (&RS)	Department of Transport (& Regional Services)
DP1	Decision point – 1 engine operating
DPA	Decision point – all engines operating
DPD	Decision point – depressurised
DPE	Decision point – ETOPS
EASA	European Union Aviation Safety Agency
ECC	Emergency control centre
EDTO	Extended diversion time operations
EET	Estimated elapsed time
EFB	Electronic flight bag
ELBA	Emergency location beacon – aircraft
ELT	Emergency locator transmitter
EMS	Emergency medical services
EPs	Emergency procedures
EROPS	Extended range operations
ETA	Estimated time of arrival
ETD	Estimated time of departure
ETOPS	Extended twin engine operations
EZFW	Estimated zero fuel weight
FAA	Federal Aviation Administration
FAAA	Flight Attendants' Association of Australia
FAF	Final approach fix
FAM	Flight administration manual
FANS	Future air navigation system
FDPS	Flight data processing system
FFR	Fixed fuel reserve
FIC	Flight information centre
FIFO	Fly in – fly out
FIR	Flight information region
FIS	Flight information service
FL	Flight level
FMS	Flight management system
FMU	Flow management unit
FOD	Fuel over destination
FOQA	Flight operations quality assurance
FPL	Flight plan

COMMON ABBREVIATIONS

FPO	Freight planning office
FRMS	Fatigue risk-management system
FSO	Flight standing order
FTB	Failed to board (passenger)
FTD	Fleet team digest
FTI	Flight time interval
GA	General aviation
GDP	General data processing
GE	General Electric
GOC	Ground operations coordinator
GPS	Global positioning system
GRANDFATHER RIGHTS	A provision for continuation of an old rule or situation with exemption given should a new rule apply to future cases
HF	High frequency (radio)
HIAL	High intensity approach lighting
IAS	Indicated air speed
IATA	International Air Transport Association
ICAO	International Civil Aviation Organisation
IFR	Instrument flight rules
ILS	Instrument landing system
IMC	Instrument meteorological conditions
INCERFA	Uncertainty phase
INS	Inertial navigation system
INTAM	Internal notice to airmen
INTER	Intermittent weather period
IOC	Integrated Operations Centre
ISS	In-flight service schedule
IVOL	Volcanic update
kg	Kilogram
LAHSO	Land and hold short operations
LIR	Load instruction report
LOSA	Line operations safety audit
LPATS	Lightning, position & tracking system
LTOP	Long-term operating plan
MAC	Mean aerodynamic cord
MAYDAY	Distress signal – aircraft in grave or imminent danger – needs immediate assistance
MBRW	Maximum brakes release weight

COMMON ABBREVIATIONS

MBZ	Mandatory broadcast zone
MEL	Minimum equipment list
MET	Meteorology
METAR	Aviation routine weather (WX) report
MINIMA	Approved cloud base and visibility for actual approach and landing
MLW	Maximum landing weight
MOC	Maintenance Operations Centre
MOG	Meal on ground
MTOW	Maximum take-off weight
NATS	National Air Traffic Services Agency (UK)
NCC	Network Control Centre
NDB	Non-directional beacon (radio)
NM	Nautical miles
NOC	Network Operations Control/Centre
NOSIG	No significant change
NOTAM	Notice to airmen
NOTOC	Notification to Captain of special load
OCC	Operations Control Centre
OEW	Operating empty weight
OFTS	Overseas fixed telecommunications system
OGS	Operational group schedules
OOOI	Out, off, on, in
OPS CTRL	Operations Control
OTP	On-time performance
PAN	Urgent message re safety of A/C or person (lower priority than mayday)
PAPI	Precision approach path indicator
PBCF	Performance-based contingency fuel
PDC	Pre-departure clearance
PIC	Persons in custody
PIC	Pilot in Command
PIREP	Pilot report
PNR	Point of no return
PRM	Precision runway monitoring
PSM	Passenger services manager
PTL	Planned time of landing
PTS	Precision timing schedule
QNH	Atmospheric pressure adjusted to mean sea level
QRH	Quick reference handbook
RCLM	Runway centre-line marking

COMMON ABBREVIATIONS

(A) RFF	(Aviation) Rescue and fire fighting
RLC	Regionalised Load Control
RMS	Route manual supplement
RNAV	Area navigation
RNP-AR	Required navigation performance – authorisation required
ROC	Regional Operations Control/Centre
RPT	Regular public transport
RTO	Rejected take-off
RVR	Runway visual range
RVSM	Reduced vertical separation minimum
RWY	Runway
SAR	Search and rescue
SATCOM	Satellite communication
SCR	Schedule change request
SELCAL	Selective calling system
SG	Specific gravity
SID	Standard instrument departure
SIGMET	Significant meteorological (info. concerning en-route weather which may affect safety of aircraft)
SIGWX	Significant weather
SIS	Security & investigation services
SITA	Société International Télégraphique Aéronautique
SLAM	Special low alternate minimum
SLOTCO	Slots Coordinator
SNOWTAM	NOTAM notifying the presence or removal of hazardous conditions due to snow, ice or slush on runway
SOCC	Systems Operations Control Centre
SPECI	Aviation special weather
SSB	Single sideband
STA	Scheduled time of arrival
STAR	Standard arrival route
STD	Scheduled time of departure
TAC	Turnaround coordinator
TAF/TAFOR	Terminal area forecast
TAMP	Terminal area management plan
TAS	True air speed
TCAS	Traffic collision avoidance system
TCRF/FCRF	Technical crew/flight crew rest facility
TDZ	Touchdown zone

COMMON ABBREVIATIONS

TEMPO	Temporary weather period
TIBA	Traffic information broadcast by aircraft
TOC	Top of climb
ToD	Tour of duty
TOD	Top of descent
TODA	Take-off distance available
TORA	Take-off run available
TOW	Take-off weight
UHF	Ultra-high frequency
UPR	User preferred routes
UTC	Universal time coordinate (Zulu)
VASI	Visual approach slope indicator
VFR	Variable fuel reserve
VFR	Visiting friends and relatives
VFR	Visual flight rules
VHF	Very high frequency (radio)
VIP	Very important person
VMC	Visual meteorological conditions
VMO	Maximum operating speed
VNAV	Vertical navigation
VOLMET	Meteorological info. for A/C in flight
VOR	VHF omnidirectional radio range
WIP	Work(s) in progress
WPT	Waypoint
WX	Weather
ZFW	Zero fuel weight

ENGINEERING

ACARS	Aircraft communication addressing and reporting system
ACM	Air cycle machine
ACMP	Alternating current motor pump
AD	Airworthiness directive
ADF	Automatic direction finder
ADI	Attitude direction indicator
ADP	Air driven pump
AH	Artificial horizon
AICC	A/C interior compliance check

COMMON ABBREVIATIONS

AME	Aircraft maintenance engineer
AOA	Angle of attack
AOG	Aircraft on ground
APU	Auxiliary power unit
ASI	Air speed indicator
ATP	Authority to proceed
ATS	Automatic throttle system
BITE	Built in test equipment
BLG	Body landing gear
BPCU	Bus power control unit
CAMEO	Combined aircraft maintenance and engineering orders system
CAMSYS	Combined aircraft maintenance systems
CB	Circuit breaker
CDI	Course deviation indicator
CDL	Configuration deviation list
CDS	Common display unit
CDU	Centre drive unit
CDU	Control display units
CFR	Cabin focus revue
CONFIG	Configuration
CPCS	Cabin pressure control system
CSD	Constant speed drive
CVR	Cockpit voice recorder
CWT	Centre wing tank
DADC	Digital air data computer
DDG	Dispatch deviation guide
DFDR	Digital flight data recorder
EA	Engineering authority
EADI	Electronic attitude director indicator
ECAMs	Electronic centralised aircraft monitor
EDFP	Engine driven fuel pump
EDHP	Engine driven hydraulic pump
EDP	Engine driven pump
EEC	Electronic engine control
EFIS	Electronic flight instrument system
EGT	Exhaust gas temperature
EHSI	Electronic horizontal situation indicator
EICAS	Engine indication & crew alerting system
EIS	Engineering instruction sheet
EIU	Electronic interface unit

COMMON ABBREVIATIONS

EOC	Engine overhaul centre
EPR	Engine pressure ratio
ETOMS	Engineering technical options management systems
ETS	Estimated time of serviceability
FADEC	Full authority digital engine control
FAFC	Full authority fuel control
FCC	Flight control computer
FCU	Flight control unit
FDR	Flight data recorder
FFR	Fuel flow regulator
FIM	Flight isolation manual
FMC	Flight management computer
FMU	Fuel metering unit
FOD	Foreign object damage
FQIS	Fuel quantity indicating system
FRM	Fault reporting manual
FSEU	Flap slat electronic unit
GCU	Generator control unit
GE	General Electric
GPU	Ground power unit
GPWS	Ground proximity warning system
GTCP	Gas turbine compressor power
HMG	Hydraulic motor generator
HPC	High-pressure compressor
HPT	High-pressure turbine
HSI	Horizontal situation indicator
HST	Horizontal stabiliser tank
HUD	Heads up display
IDG	Integrated drive generator
IFE	In-flight entertainment
IFSD	In-flight shutdown
INOP	Inoperative
INU	Inertial navigation unit
IRS	Inertial reference system
IRU	Inertial reference unit
ISE	In seat entertainment
IVSI	Integrated vertical speed indicator
LAME	Licensed aircraft maintenance engineer
MCD	Mag chip detector
MDO	Must do
MEC	Main engine control

COMMON ABBREVIATIONS

MEC	Main equipment centre
MEL	Minimum equipment list
MIM	Maintenance instruction manual
MLG	Main landing gear
MOC DM	Maintenance Operations Duty Manager
NDI	Non-destructive inspection
NGV	Nozzle guide vane
NLG	Nose landing gear
ONS	Overnight service (typically 2130–0630 local time)
OSIP	Overhaul special inspection period
PAG	Pump and governor
PCA	Power control actuators
PDU	Power driven unit
PRSOV	Pressure regulating & shutoff valve
PRV	Pressure regulating valve
PSCCA	Pax seat condition check
PSCU	Pax seat control unit
PSEU	Pax services entertainment unit
PSEU	Proximity switch electronics unit
PSI	Pounds per square inch
PSU	Passenger service unit
PTU	Power transfer unit
QAR	Quick access recorder
RAT	Ram air turbine
SAT	Static air temperature
SRM	Structural repair manual
TAS	True air speed
TAT	Total air temperature
TCAS	Traffic collision avoidance system
TRU	Transformer rectifier units
TX	Time expired
U/S	Unserviceable
VIGV	Variable inlet guide vanes
VSI	Vertical speed indicator
VSV	Variable stator vanes
WLG	Wing landing gear

SECURITY

CERP	Corporate emergency response plan
DSC	Duty Security Controller
EAT	Emergency assessment team
ECC	Emergency control centre
IRIT	Immediate response investigation team
PTI	Positive target identification
REACT	Reservations emergency air incident control team
SAT	Special assistance team
TAT	Threat assessment team

PREFACE

The purpose of this book is to provide an in-depth look within the nerve centre of an airline; typically referred to as its Operations Control Centre (OCC), or an equivalent name chosen by an airline to manage this crucially important aspect of its business (see *Terminology* later in this chapter). Aviation is a highly complex, dynamic, and very exciting industry. In this environment, safety is absolutely crucial, and non-negotiable, and in this text the words that follow are founded well and truly upon this mandate. With this always in mind, airlines operate within very tight legal, financial and economic margins in an environment fraught with complex operational challenges and disruptions. To exist and prosper in such an environment requires appropriate managerial and domain expertise, state-of-the-art facilities, and sophisticated systems and procedures. To meet an airline's operational objectives, efficient and responsible operational control is charged to a central body of highly skilled and expert practitioners. It is their world that this book explores.

The book is designed primarily for practitioners; those whose interests or career paths may lie within, across, or otherwise be connected with, the operational side of the airline business with the focus clearly on the activities of the core or central operational entity. There are two distinctive parts to the book. In Part I, Chapter 1 describes and explains the Operations Centre, the reason for its existence, purpose and philosophy and structural characteristics. Chapter 2 focuses on the key people who operate within the centre, in particular explaining the characteristics and skill-sets of the person needed for the crucial role of Operations Controller and postulating some guidance to assist airline management in the recruitment, selection, and training of appropriate individuals. One of the aims of this chapter is to provide airline management with a sound appreciation of the disposition of person needed for this role. The chapter also explains the numerous internal and external relationships common to many OCCs. Chapter 3 considers the extensiveness of activities leading to the day of operation. The chapter explains the business, commercial and operational factors that influence operational planning

PREFACE

and preparation, as well as many of the actions undertaken by related functional departments that precede the handover leading to daily operational control. The final chapter in Part I explains the variety of sophisticated systems and tools in place within an OCC to enable it to function. This chapter also depicts the processes occurring within the Operations Centre with in-depth explanations of regular and irregular operations and the methods by which disruptions may be managed. The chapter elucidates the ways in which Operations Controllers go about their tasks.

Part II builds on this framework and background material, applying the concepts therein to real-world situations. Thus, the aim in the second part of the book is to examine an extensive range of representative operational disruptions and focus systematically on the cognitive processes of Controllers tasked with managing such problems. The chapters consider four real-life scenarios. Chapter 5 bridges the gap from the more foundational Part I of the book, by demonstrating how the concepts of decision making and problem solving an aircraft engineering issue actually translate in terms of notifications and advanced thought processes within the Integrated Operations Centre (IOC), the various interactions and communications with key stakeholders, and the methods used to analyse, act and recover from the disruption. In each of Chapters 6, 7 and 8, a detailed scenario has been constructed to represent a typical airline disruption that might occur in different parts of the world. The scenarios are structured methodically and consistently to illustrate the various steps involved in the decision-making process, such as accumulating and enhancing situation awareness through information acquisition, communicating with various functional areas, assessing decision alternatives, reaching final deliberation and disseminating decisions appropriately. To augment this process, progressive graphical displays are placed, where possible, on the facing page to enhance the commentary and illustrate the evolving solution to the problem, while in the text, icons are used to signify the information transfers, thought processes and actions occurring within the IOC. In this way, the reader can gain a deeper understanding of the emerging issues and considerations taken into account for optimal decision making and problem resolution.

Readers of this book, no matter their role within or external to the airline industry, or even their current role within another operational environment, may well be surprised to discover the nature and intensity of work undertaken in the Operations Centre, so the intention here is to familiarise the reader with the vast array of problems typically encountered in airline operations and articulate the thought processes necessary to resolve these problems while optimising operational efficiency and performance.

Part I

OPERATIONS FUNCTION

1 OPERATIONS CONTROL

INTRODUCTION

This chapter will introduce and describe the concept of, and the rationale underpinning, the Airline Operations Control Centre (OCC), its purpose for existence and its importance in airline usage. The structure, siting and make-up of the centre all vary considerably in terms of physical layout, complexity and participation by contributing players. A focus of the chapter will be to examine the associations among these players as well as their external affiliations, as the building and maintaining of close working relationships are key to efficient problem recognition and solving.

Regulatory Framework

Although it is beyond the scope of this text to delve deeply into the regulatory specifics relating to operational control, it is nevertheless important and relevant to provide a basic framework. The need for operational control is recognised in a number of ways. First is to define the term 'operational control'. According to Chapter 1 of Annex 6 to the Chicago Convention, operational control refers to 'the exercise of authority over the initiation, continuation, diversion or termination of a flight in the interests of the safety of the aircraft, and the regularity and efficiency of the flight'.[1] Thus, operational control relates to all phases of a flight. Chapter 3 of the Annex also clarifies that the operator or its delegate is responsible for operational control. The Operations Control Centre (OCC) then (or whatever name an airline uses) assumes the responsibility for operational control on behalf of the airline. It is important to note that the OCC needs to conform to regulations not only at international level, but must also take into account national government regulations of each State (as defined by the International Civil Aviation Organisation – ICAO) into which operations are conducted, and be fully aware that these regulations can and do vary between States. These pertain, for example, to such areas as crew duty hours, requirements for maintaining flight watch, as well as numerous requirements regarding engineering activities.

Within the OCC, the tasks of operational control are then delegated to roles such as, for example, an Operations Controller (so called in many jurisdictions) or Dispatcher, as in the case of the licensed Dispatcher (see *Flight Dispatch* in the next chapter). Beside the airline's legal requirement to provide operational control, a key objective of the OCC is to satisfy commercial expectations (i.e., conduct of a schedule as advertised to, and expected by, its customers and other stakeholders). Hence, the OCC is tasked with ensuring the network of schedules is achieved as closely as possible to the planned operation. How it accomplishes this is then the focus of both the current and following chapters.

Terminology

Several terms have been used to describe an airline's Operations Centre. The obvious and probably most commonly used has been, and still is, the OCC or perhaps the AOC (Airline Operations Control). Some airlines, though, have preferred AOCC (Airline Operations Control Centre), SOCC (Systems Operations Control Centre), NCC (Network Control Centre), or NOC (Network Operations Centre), while some smaller airlines may use the term ROC (Regional Operations Control or Centre). More recently, and for very good reason, the participation and structural inclusion of a growing number of key departments within the Operations Centre has led to the evolvement and formation, and hence terminology, of the Integrated Operations Centre or IOC. The term 'integrated' is deliberate to emphasise the synthesis of purpose and activity contained within the one authority. This organisational entity has developed significantly over time and its key role in handling the airline's operational movements can never be overstated. With full recognition of airlines' preferences and rationale of terminology in mind, the term IOC will be used throughout this text (apart from the historical perspectives below) to refer generically to any airline's OCC or system, to avoid any confusion.

DEFINING THE IOC

As discussed above, there is a regulatory requirement for an airline to conduct operational control. There is also a fundamental need for over-sight of the airline's planned network flight schedules on a day-to-day basis to ensure the actual operation mirrors as closely as possible the schedule that was intended for operation. Of course, the schedule is what has been presented to, and is therefore relied upon by, the trav-elling public. Whether an airline is a small charter or regional carrier with a minimal number of aircraft, or a major company with hundreds of aircraft and a sophisticated network of operations spanning several countries, the necessity for a 'nerve centre' with responsibility for the legal, safe and efficient operation of the fleet is manifest. Thus, airlines manage their operational control through this centralised department. The centre is tasked with monitoring the airline's diversity of flights from pre-planning, departure, en route, and arrival stages, for its entire network, handling not only regular, scheduled services,[2] but charters and special operations as required. IOCs are unique to each airline. Each is differently structured, has its own systems, procedures and policies, and culture. Of course, each airline's network is also unique – no two airlines in the world have the same route structure or fleet composition. So the IOC is built specifically to drive the goals of its own airline.

Besides this role to coordinate and manage the airline's operational activity, the IOC serves another key function within the airline. Its centrality, elaborate structure, inclusive representation and extensive reach into many areas of the operation give it unique characteristics. Nowhere else in an airline is a department more in touch with the occurrence of operational events, and with other participating stakeholders. Accordingly, the IOC is a natural hub of communication. External parties can access and listen in to events unfolding or provide advice as required. Outward communications can also be readily disseminated to a wide range of recipients.

In the event of a significant abnormal or extraordinary incident which may evolve into a crisis situation (e.g., security, safety or otherwise), the initial handling of the event will most likely be managed by the IOC. However, the severity of an emerging situation will determine the extent to which the IOC will continue to manage it, as its impact may require dedicated attention either for a short duration, or if a major event, a substantial length of time. Hence, management of such an event may well be given to an offshoot of the IOC such as a crisis management centre, which is usually physically located away from the IOC and is typically comprised of specialist team members including senior management, experts from various key functional areas of the airline, other nominated airline personnel and external authorities as required. Part of the team will include specialist expertise representation from the IOC itself. It is important to recognise that alongside an emerging crisis (depending on its nature and gravity), the balance of the airline's network is likely to be unaffected by the specific event, and therefore still needs to be managed. In other words, the IOC still needs to continue its normal activity.

HISTORY

In decades past, many departmental areas of an airline functioned somewhat independently. Essentially, they operated largely in terms of a silo-based mindset, tasked with their own objectives and goals, and complete with singular departmental metrics to gauge their own performance and results. Staff in these units often had little or no concept of occurrences outside their own area of work, often limited knowledge of other departments and the work carried out within them, and only a modest understanding of the extent to which each may influence the other.

Hence, the impact of decisions in some areas was not well appreciated or comprehended in others. It was a most dysfunctional structure. In these times too, before the relative 'explosion' of air travel that was to take place in later decades, there were few competing interests. The regulatory environment restricted competition, there was minimal airport and airspace congestion and Air Traffic Control operated with vastly simpler equipment and procedures, than today. Fuel was relatively plentiful and other than during identified, recurring periods of world tension, was reasonably priced. Governments often supported or owned airlines, and the cost to do business was less questioned or at least was not under the spotlight anywhere near as much as today.

OCC CONSIDERATIONS

The early years

The OCC as it was then more commonly termed, was no exception. It was often an area hidden away within an airline, seemingly unknown, certainly misunderstood, often mistrusted, and considered by senior management as a cost function to the bottom line of the business. As such, management had no appetite to invest in improving the operational centre. Without due recognition, investment for improvements to operational systems, communications tools, and appropriate staff recruitment and training, was not forthcoming. In addition, the tools in the OCC were often individually sourced and used in isolation for single tasks. They were technologically diverse, often obtained from an array of suppliers with vested interests in specific aspects of the operation (such as for Aircraft Movements, Crewing Resource Planning, or Reservations functions), but lacking the scope and capability to present as unified packages. This resulted, for example, in the Aircraft Movements system not 'communicating with' the Crewing system, or the Reservations system. This lack of system integration and cohesion caused much frustration, increased workloads, and inefficiencies in the way in which the OCC was able to operate, and certainly became a growing concern for cost control.

Of course, once these individual systems were selected and ensconced in the day-to-day operation, their use became the norm, with greater reliance by staff, and with little incentive to change what appeared to work well (albeit independently). As a result, the financial (and social) cost of replacing them to enable improved standardisation, or better still, synthesis, became prohibitive such that there developed a sustained existence of numerous, stand-alone programs. Notwithstanding systems shortfalls, of course in these times there was no internet in existence, so access to, and gathering of, reliable information to aid decision making, and then communicating and disseminating the results was a slow process. Travel agents dominated and so were relied upon to service passenger bookings and journey management, and the passenger was largely in the hands of these systems. Booking conditions were quite strict as well, with economic penalties for booking one-way, requirements for minimum stay, and often inclusion of specific days (e.g., Saturday) to receive discounted packages. Passengers had little choice and certainly no self-input into booking processes.

The problem-solving process was highly reactive; typically applying a 'fire-fighting' approach as the OCC responded to situations as they evolved, and hence recovery was highly reactionary and somewhat routine. During these times, a blame culture mentality was evident. As functional areas largely operated independently, an attitude of 'XYZ have done this or that' was quite prevalent, and other areas would feel obliged to 'fix' problems created elsewhere. In this era, of course, there was less competition, but the downside of that was that there was also less choice to assist in providing viable solutions (e.g., uplift of disrupted passengers on the airline's own flights or those of other carriers). Solutions were to a large degree 'hull' focused, rather than customer focused, meaning that disruption solutions were predicated more on salvaging aircraft patterns than they were on mitigating the effects on passenger trips. Even the terminology 'passenger' used in the earlier days was attitudinally differently from the terms 'customer' or 'guest' more commonly in use today. In these earlier days, load factors (i.e., the proportion of occupied seats to total aircraft capacity) were typically light, and with frequencies of flights being fewer, disruption recovery was relatively straightforward. Disrupted passengers were often accommodated when they could be – usually on 'later' flights, even sometimes having to be uplifted the following day or, worse, when a service was next scheduled (and even then, one having sufficient seats for carriage). Low-cost carriers, as we know them today, had either not emerged in the early years, or were just starting to take a foothold.

Into the 21st century

In the 1990s and 2000s, many evolutionary changes occurred in the industry. The prevalence of low-cost carriers was materialising, leading to rapid changes in competition, and driving costs down. Linked strongly with this was the change to airline ownership, with many governments divesting themselves of involvement with their national airlines. With the subsequent 'explosion' in air travel, congestion started to become a major problem in numerous regions of the world. Airports expanded to cope with greater demand, and secondary airports began to gain acceptance, developing greater infrastructure to handle growing domestic needs, and often facilitating international services.

Activity within the OCC steadily became more system focused, as changes in technology materialised. Software vendors either realised the potential, or were driven by the airlines themselves, to focus on providing these developments, such that tools emerged to enhance the usefulness of graphical displays available to Controllers, thereby delivering greater functionality to assist in optimising disruption recovery. For example, to manage a major weather disruption (such as a blizzard or hurricane) more readily, the newer tools enabled large-scale remedies affecting high numbers of flight stages to be enacted in a shorter timeframe, resulting in faster recovery, and a reduction in the workloads of Controllers. Technological improvements also contributed to more coordinated approaches among functional areas, especially those with engineering, commercial and operational interests, and a joint problem-solving culture developed. Thus, a transition from self-satisfying departmental pursuits to airline-focused, integrated decision outcomes began to emerge.

To support this approach, joint metrics were developed to measure, inform, analyse and advance systems performance, leading to innovations in planning and operating, but increasingly with a focus on continuous improvement across the board. Part of this process has seen greater attention given to revenue retention and protection, and importantly, cost control. There has also been a concerted effort to pin-point opportunities for cost reduction, particularly targeting high-cost activities such as Crewing and Maintenance resources, as well as isolating costs associated with non-core activity. As a result, productivity was increased, reductions in overheads realised, and levels of spares and inventory driven down. Outsourcing became instrumental in helping to reduce workforce size and liability. For example, maintenance repairs and overhaul, once handled in-country, could be outsourced to local third-party contractors or sent off-shore, airline workforces were downsized, and with the casualisation of the workforce, full-time employment translated to part-time or casual positions. Certainly, more flexibility in employment agreements was becoming necessary to enable substantial change to the way in which work was done.

What was significantly changing over this time was the re-focusing on customers and analysis of their relative worth to the company. A lot of this was fed by awareness of growing competition, not only in terms of the number of new airlines and therefore much greater choice for the travelling public, but in terms of evolving state-of-the-art aircraft, with sophisticated premium cabins in many cases, offering an extensive display of product and service. Far more choice and the fact that customers can readily take their business elsewhere with little or no penalty have been some of the drivers of the re-focus on the customer journey. Thus, customer impact has become increasingly central to operational decision making, especially with regard to high-value customers in premium class travel or those with high-standing loyalty (either from their home or primary carrier, or from alliance and partner airlines).

DRIVERS OF CHANGE IN THE IOC

Several factors have been responsible for the philosophical changes in the IOC itself. First, senior airline management have come to realise the vital role played by the IOC in managing the airline's assets; a philosophical move away from the perception of the IOC as more of a derivation of costs. Given the ability to touch many parts of the airline in the natural course of its day, the IOC is now recognised as having significant 'feel' for airline behaviour and performance. In addition, there is true acceptance by the airline of the vital contribution of the IOC to the bottom line. It has become a centre of excellence. Second, as a nucleus for information and communications, and through its ability to exercise positive control over the airline, the IOC has become a key driver of outcomes crucial to airline performance. It can harness and coordinate a wide range of resources leading to greater efficiencies in the operational space. It can also play its part in helping to drive down operational costs, for example, through better informed and quicker decision-making processes, or the instigation of instruments such as fuel policies to optimise fuel carriage and burn, or perhaps protect against shortages or threats to supply.

As part of its own review of performance, the IOC is able to critique the roles of its membership. For example, it is well placed to influence policy, lobby for changes to crew availability, rostering or rest practices, improvements to schedule, or demands for additional ground resources, as a result of identifying causes underlying or exacerbating disruptions. To substantiate proposals such as these, it now has at hand significant data and other supporting evidence to argue its case.

TOWARD CUSTOMER CENTRICITY

Airline customers understand that at some point in their travel, they are likely to be disrupted. How the airline responds and recovers customer journeys, and in the process, how it treats its customers, are increasingly critical for the reputation of the airline and vital for retaining a loyal customer base. With this renewed emphasis, the focus of the IOC has well and truly been directed toward customer satisfaction. In this digital age, the need for faster and more appropriate decisions, together with optimal solutions that impact the paying public less, have been realised in response to mounting customer pressure. Customers now are not only aware of disruptions as they are occurring, but through social media platforms they can generate and broadcast information as events first materialise or unfold, and then, to a vast worldly audience (including the media). More than ever, they want instant solutions and prompt actions should their travel plans be upset. With their renewed customer focus, IOCs increasingly are now able to do just this. They can respond to situations more efficiently, producing better decision outcomes and disseminating the necessary information through sophisticated communications channels. In a way, what used to take 24 hours may now take 24 seconds. This has a significant impact on the travelling public, provided the customer-recovery processes are sincere in their efforts.

INFLUENCE OF SOCIAL MEDIA

A number of communications platforms have become commonplace on board aircraft. Many airlines have introduced, then enhanced the availability and capability of WIFI, giving passengers real-time information at their fingertips, thus providing them with the ability to remain current with world events. The opportunities this technology provides to enable such communication raise potential issues faced by airlines, such as those concerning security, ethics, confidentiality, or the transmission of socially inappropriate material. With the rapid expansion and influence of social media platforms, airlines have become well aware of the speed and distribution of social messaging in relation to their performance, levels of service, on-board incidents and other events, whether these communiqués are negative or positive. Suddenly, airborne communications systems virtually anywhere in the world enable rapid contact with any other party in the world.

Accordingly, many IOCs have embedded social media representation within their centres to maximise awareness of current public sentiment.

OPERATIONS CONTROL

Indeed, on occasions, first advice of a situation may be observed through this channel before official intelligence is received. The social media staff monitor a wide range of occurrences on a 24/7 basis to provide real-time information to the IOC, enabling it to respond as necessary. This ongoing process has become a valuable tool for the IOC to waylay misconceptions, ward off negative comment, or simply respond to questions, and the communications can be forwarded broadly or specifically directed to key stakeholders within the airline.

The pattern of influence may also be used another way. Once aware of an impending upset such as a delay or cancellation, for example, the IOC now has the means to be highly proactive, and broadcast intentions via its own social media function prior to individual customers taking their own particular course of action, thereby offering rapid and opportune communication among the airline's customer base. Even more significant now, is the opportunity for the Customer Journey Management (CJM) team within the IOC to forewarn identified customers about a looming disruption, alerting them perhaps to the need to arrive or check-in early at the airport (or not to travel at all). In some cases, customers may already have been moved onto alternate services. This is a most positive aspect of social media. Customers can be pinpointed according to flight(s), or port of disruption, or by previous recognition per a VIP or CIP (commercially important person) list. This approach to customer journey management charges the IOC with a powerful means of customer benefit not available previously.

LOCATION

The actual location of an airline's IOC is, ironically, not crucial. However, access to appropriate corporate staff, and the numerous affiliated departments that depend on, and/or influence operational processes, really determines the optimum locale for such a key department. Hence, IOCs tend to be established within or close to the airline's head office in a major city or airport, and in particular, the airline's main hub. While city locations may facilitate corporate access when needed, the proximity to crucial operational resources (such as Pilot and Flight Attendant Scheduling, Maintenance Control, Airport and Ground-Handling personnel) may be regarded as more advantageous. Hence, they are often but not always sited at, or close to, an airport environment. Physically, the IOC is assembled on one or more floors within a state-of-the-art, secure building, in which access is usually restricted to appropriate personnel. The evolving IOC over years has drawn several different functional areas into the core group, which has resulted in a physical structure of considerable size.

In some large airlines, a fit-for-purpose building houses the IOC functions usually in some form of concentric design or similar array over one floor, with oversight provided for senior duty management via a raised bridge or platform area. Crucial on-the-day decision makers are located closest to the centre, with more supportive or resource-based roles positioned further away. This sort of clustered structure lends itself to high noise volumes in times of intense activity, but the close proximity of key areas far outweighs any disadvantages due to the critical nature of shared problem awareness, dynamic information, and collaborative decision making. To provide redundancy due to power or systems failures, or perhaps due to any situations of a security or other nature, an alternative or back-up IOC is sited at a different location. Although the back-up centre may not comprise the same infrastructure and layout as the main one, it needs to be capable of providing full operational control until activity in the main centre can be resumed. Temporary transfer of control to the back-up centre is usually tested annually or biennially.

PURPOSE AND PHILOSOPHY

The prime purpose of the IOC is to oversee the provision of the end-to-end customer experience and meet each customer's expectation for a safe, legal and efficient flight from point A to point B. Safety is paramount in the industry and any airline that does not subscribe to the highest levels of safety is in the wrong business. Legality refers to the myriad regulations that determine the means by which airlines operate and the need for compliance across licensing, operating standards and procedures, maintenance, and service provision, for example. These occur at international and national governmental levels as well as at airline policy level. Efficiency implies that the airline will achieve schedule integrity through delivery of on-time performance, and in doing so, will deploy resources judiciously to ensure their optimal utility, while maximising revenues and containing costs. Cost control, as mentioned earlier, has become of immense concern given rising charges across industry (e.g., fuel, aircraft purchases, salaries, landing fees and overflight charges), increased competition, stakeholder interests, and a continual focus on the bottom line.

Considerable and widespread planning processes determine the state of readiness of the airline as the day of operation approaches. But of course, despite these efforts, no airline schedule operates exactly as planned, and disruptions need to be very carefully managed to mitigate their effects on both immediate and intending customers. The ways in which the IOC goes about this are many and varied, reliant on a combination of highly skilled, expert staff, the philosophical approach to delivering customer service, and the innumerable constraints accountable within the decision-making processes. Where possible, the IOC operates proactively by forecasting and acting upon potential disruptions, thereby averting threats to the network, but much of the nature of their work is reactive, requiring rapid assessment, precise communication and efficient resolution of situations. Thus, the aims are twofold: first to resolve problems, and second to connect effectively with both internal and external stakeholders. To satisfy the relationships among the IOC team and others, the user investment in the IOC is rewarded by a strategy of sound communications and reporting procedures.

AUTONOMY

No matter what reporting channels are employed, a key necessity for an IOC is for a high degree of impartiality and autonomy required for operational oversight and management. Interwoven with this is the key to the IOC model: that is, the necessity for the innermost group to have authority for decision making within their own jurisdictions on the day of operations. If individuals cannot make authorised decisions without having to refer to more senior personnel within their functional areas, then the inclusion of those individuals in the IOC is valueless, as decision making in such a complex and challenging environment cannot be served by a committee approach. Given this authority, so it is that the centre operates with a suitable level of independence, and any undue interference in operational decision processes is prevented. Of course, this is not to say that the IOC operates in isolation; far from it. The nature of the IOC demands that close and intense communications with key stakeholders from various areas both within and external to the airline, inform its processes appropriately. But crucially, this communication is two-way. Of course, the IOC needs to gather accurate, reliable and timely intelligence to underpin its decision-making processes, but also needs to disseminate outcomes and associated information promptly to a wide range of stakeholders. In disruption management, the window of opportunity may often be quite narrow, so the need to channel communications promptly and concisely is critical.

Hierarchy and Reporting Lines

The IOC usually is contained within a larger departmental structure variously called Central or Network Operations and, occasionally, the IOC may be part of a Flight Operations Department. Direct reporting lines may be to a Vice President–Operations, an Operations Director or General Manager–Operations, or perhaps Flight Operations Manager depending upon the company structure. Whatever the size and make-up of the operational structure, reporting lines need to be unambiguous and ensure that efficient communication channels enable appropriate paths for advice seeking and direction setting. The individual titles and reporting lines may vary, but notably, the tasks still need to be performed in some way.

Notes

1 ICAO ANNEX 6: Operation of aircraft, Part I – International Commercial Air transport – Aeroplanes. 10th ed. July 2016. Viewed 10/03/20. www. universiteitleiden.nl/binaries/content/assets/rechtsgeleerdheid/instituut-voor-publiekrecht/lucht--en-ruimterecht/international-air-law-moot-court/annex-6_part-i.pdf
2 Abdi, M.R., and Sharma, S. 2007. Strategic/tactical information management of flight operations in abnormal conditions through Network Control Centre. *International Journal of Information Management*, 27, 119–138.

2 COMPOSITION OF THE IOC

INTRODUCTION

The composition of the IOC is somewhat determined by the size and complexity of the airline. A small, regional airline may well feature a range of multi-skilled professionals including Operations Controllers, Operations Officers, or Dispatchers (see below) who could find themselves responsible for aircraft movements as well as looking after crew rostering and resourcing tasks, scheduling, and many other activities. The facility may be quite small and, as a result, is not likely to include many of the more formal functional areas typically found in larger centres. It can be soon realised that individuals in these small centres need to be highly adept in a range of activities, have broad, but detailed knowledge across several specialist areas, and communicate extensively across the airline at many levels.

In contrast, in the larger centres typically found in major airlines, the diversity of staff and professions multiplies accordingly. In these centres, expertise is far more specialised, and corresponding with functional activities such as Operations (or Movements) Control, Dispatch, Crew Resources, Crew Planning, Engineering (Maintenance Watch/Control), CJM, Airport Coordination, Slot Management, Meteorology, and so forth. With this degree of specialisation, so greater levels of expertise are needed. Dealing with regulatory limitations, and Pilot or Flight Attendant industrial awards, for example, calls for meticulous knowledge and a proven ability to interpret and apply rules in order to manage high levels of complexity. In this environment, the risk of incorrect application may have significant ramifications for the airline. Following is a break-down and description of the key components of the IOC and their roles, with a particular emphasis on the role of Operations Controller. Some IOCs may not include some of the functions described, while others include more such roles or perhaps describe them under different names.

OPERATIONS CONTROL FUNCTION

The Operations Control function (sometimes referred to as *movements control* or *aircraft control*) often takes the dominant focus in the IOC. It is usually physically located in the centre of the IOC in order for it to be determined and regarded as the nucleus of activity, enabling ready communications with key functional areas, and drawing upon the expertise around it for a collaborative approach to problem solving. Notably, there are variances between IOCs in terms of the titles of staff and the functions carried out by individuals. Operations Controllers in some jurisdictions such as the USA, are effectively Aircraft Movements Controllers (alternatively called *routers*), responsible primarily for monitoring and manipulating aircraft patterns, perhaps identifying opportunities to swap aircraft registrations/tail numbers as required, and involved in liaising with Ramp Dispatch, Load Control, Engineering, Crewing, Slot Control, and Flow Management, for example. However, outside these jurisdictions, the Controllers command greater input and decision participation. Due to the size of some airline fleets, the Operations Control function is often divided to limit the number of flights under the control of individuals. This division of responsibility may result in allocating control of flights corresponding to long-haul or short-haul operations, according to international and domestic purpose, or by some system of segregation into geographical regions. Further break-down may correlate to fleet type. As this text is intentionally focused on the Operations Control function, the roles, characteristics and personal attributes needed for this task are discussed in considerable detail below.

IOC SENIOR MANAGEMENT

The senior management structure of the IOC will form some sort of hierarchy, with the highest level (often referred to as one of Vice President (VP), Director, Group Manager, or Head of Operations) usually reporting direct to the CEO of the airline. Under that person, is often a Manager IOC or Manager–Operations, then a number of Duty Managers who oversee the day-to-day operations on rotational shift rosters. In addition, subsidiary management staff may be responsible for operational performance and analysis, systems and IT development, or other related functions. The key responsibility of IOC management is to provide safe, legal and efficient operational performance of the airline. This implies compliance with relevant aviation legislation (worldwide and also with regard to the State within which the airline is registered), with company policy and practice, and with various industrial awards applicable to staff and other personnel. While this text recognises a more extensive hierarchy that comprises the airline's operational control division and notes the disposition and responsibilities of the senior management team, its focus predominantly lies with the management of the day-to-day operation. Thus, when considering the conduct of the Operations Control function, the scope is upwardly limited to the level of IOC Duty Manager (see below); the most senior position *on shift* that has direct bearing on the daily operational activity across the whole of the IOC. This will define the extent of the cohort appropriately.

INTERNAL RELATIONSHIPS

If the IOC can be envisaged as a wheel, then the hub of that wheel contains the central oversight position(s) with overall decision-making authority (such as a Duty Manager or management team), while the spokes depict the key functional areas within the entity. The success of the IOC concept has been realised due to the inclusion of key decision making, functional sections or departments. Mostly, these sections are represented in the IOC with qualified and duly authorised decision makers, with the supporting (and more extensive) groups from each section residing on the periphery. For example, there will be a number of individuals from the Technical (Pilot) Crewing and Flight Attendant Crewing sections within the IOC who have authority to make relevant decisions necessary for the day-to-day crewing operations. Other associated roles such as crew pairings or crew rostering activities, will lie outside this immediate group as these roles either occur forward of the day of operation, or fall outside the roles of decision makers handling disruptions. Similarly, other functional areas will have authorised representation close to the hub of the centre with supporting roles located nearby. The make-up of the IOC, of course, depends on the size and structure of the airline and the desire to include the various functional areas. Figure 2.1 presents a representative structure of the relationships described above. There is no preference or order implied by the positioning of each function. The important point is that the IOC is an integration of all these functions.

COMPOSITION OF THE IOC

Figure 2.1 Internal relationships of the IOC

IOC STAFF

Attention now turns to the staff allocated to the IOC with specific responsibility for managing the daily operations of the airline. The various functional areas explained above are accountable to the Duty Manager on shift, but they are also accountable within their own domains (i.e., to their own management team).

IOC Duty Manager

Overseeing the IOC is the Duty Manager, or some equivalent title. Essentially, this role is the most senior person on shift each day, in turn accountable to senior management in the IOC for the conduct of the airline's operations every day on a 24/7 basis. Bearing in mind the relationships indicated in Figure 2.1, this is the lead role with the authority for ensuring that the performance of each function within the IOC contributes capably and meaningfully to the overall operational performance and required deliverables. To achieve this, a high degree of astuteness and nous is needed to harness the considerable range of expertise residing in the component areas, given that the ability to build and maintain close working relationships is essential. This expertise is in high demand especially in times of significant disruption, where the problems are complex, time is often in short supply, decisions are of high impact, and the nature of the working environment is tense to say the least. At times, the situation may call for the Duty Manager's role to become that of an arbitrator, should collaborative but competing demands produce a deadlocked situation. On occasions like these, the role focuses on synergising the efforts, encouraging, empathising, perhaps placating where necessary, but most importantly providing strong leadership and clear direction. The role is truly on the front line.

Operational Staff

Attention is now focused upon the Operations Control staff specifically; that is, those responsible for making the myriad operational decisions. Subject to the jurisdiction of the country in which the airline is operating, many of the functions of the Operations Controller and Dispatcher are common, and may be performed by one or the other. In the immediately following sections, the characteristics and functions of each are considered in some detail. Any duplication does not take away from the fact that several tasks need to be performed and it will quickly become apparent that some functions cross over to an extent. Beyond these two roles, synopses of other roles in the IOC are described.

COMPOSITION OF THE IOC

OPERATIONS CONTROLLER

The nature of the Operations Controller (or Network Controller) role calls for a suitably skilled individual capable of performing in a high-pressure, fast paced, and complex environment. There are numerous systems and tools at hand to assist, as well as manuals, training engagements and other means for supporting the role. But even equipped with a multitude of resources, it is an extremely difficult and frustratingly long process to teach and train individuals how to be successful in the disruption-management role in order to master the techniques required for solving complex problems. This section explores the role and responsibilities in greater detail and focuses on the necessary characteristics and attributes of the individual to perform in an IOC, before considering the more managerial objectives of recruitment, selection and training.

ROLE

To avoid repetition and consolidate the various positions within the Operations Control function, the term 'role' takes into account a number of positions that fall within the Operations Control set of tasks. Thus, using this interpretation, the role described below includes some tasks undertaken by the Duty Manager, but encapsulates the tasks of the Senior Controller, Controller, Supporting Controller, and Operations Officer (or similar terms to distinguish between the various levels of personnel). In essence, the role is to monitor, control and coordinate activities associated with delivering the published schedule on a day-to-day basis for the airline's network. Operational management in the IOC includes activities related to normal and irregular operations (including crisis or emergency management), having a clear focus on the needs of customers but considering the various desired commercial and operational objectives and constraints.

RESPONSIBILITIES

Taking into consideration the inclusive titles above, the main responsibilities of the Operations Controller role are extensive. Controllers are responsible primarily for airline operational performance, encompassing the meeting of specific targets (e.g., on-time performance, efficiency, productivity) and in doing so, ensuring they adhere to regulatory requirements, airline policies and any workplace agreements. On a daily basis, more specifically, they are responsible for monitoring the actual aircraft movements (including pre-departure, departure, en-route progress and arrival), identifying variances to schedule, and resolving any problems accordingly to mitigate any potential or actual effects on the network. They are also responsible for communicating both internally within the IOC and externally, and across any level required. They must ensure that any communications received can be readily understood, interpreted and applied to a situation as necessary. Equally important is the necessity to disseminate information to key players. In addition to broadcasting decisions or advice, this may at times imply selective filtering of specific detail or judicious timing for the release of information subject to the nature of an event. Their responsibilities may extend actively to planning fleet commitments, negotiating slot times, coordinating route and overflight clearances, and organising other approvals.

THE PERSON

Who makes a good Controller? This is one of the more difficult questions to answer. It would seem apparent from preceding sections that the Controller is indeed a special person with an impressive array of skills, able to assess and deal single-handedly with any complex problem in a highly capably manner, then put into action the plan conceived, with immediate positive outcomes to solve a dilemma, and as a result, all falls back into place. In an ideal world, maybe! Realistically, though, the person does need to have exemplary skills in communication, negotiation, problem solving and management of self, others and the variety of tasks. To achieve all this requires the highest levels of personal aptitude, an uncompromising approach to attaining objectives and, at times, having to do so under considerable time constraints, and therefore, pressure.

But this is not all. The stand-out Controller has what could be described as a 'sixth sense'; a trait that sets him or her apart from others. This is an innate ability to sense anomalies, such as recognising when communications comprise mixed messages, or when a seemingly obvious solution has some latent pitfalls or undesired consequences, or that delaying a decision or an action is likely to yield further, at times quite contrary, information, and hence, results. These nuances characterise varying levels of awareness and instinct among Controllers. Colloquially speaking, it's in their DNA! They can either do it or they can't, and no amount of training substitutes sufficiently. If an IOC can populate itself

BACKGROUND AND EXPERIENCE

In the past, experience levels in an IOC were widespread, with many staff members having served stable, long-lasting careers, often in quite specialised roles but associated with IOC functions. Over this time, they amassed a wealth of knowledge and, of course, immense capability, through exposure to numerous problems and challenges. Indeed, they were revered for their command over the airline's operations as no one else really could understand the extent of the issues and, more importantly, the enormity of the effort taken to resolve complicated problems. What has changed over time has been the movement of staff, due to retirement, ill-suited appointment, or perhaps inability to cope with the extremes of pressure, mounting complexities, and increasing requirements to satisfy performance targets. Thus, the experience levels of staff within the IOC over time have been greatly diminished. Of course, part of the reason has been due to the developments in technology (e.g., smarter, more capable systems, and the digitalisation of mundane or repetitive activity) which, ironically, have also removed some fundamental or baseline understanding of the principles involved in the task. These system improvements enable tasks to be conducted more efficiently and capably, but this comes with downsides as well. First, the number of skilled staff in total has diminished, and second, the 'leg work' traditionally carried out by new staff as part of their grounded learning is now system-driven, removing this important series of progressive steps. Such shortfalls in learning and knowledge gain need to be recognised, acknowledged and compensated for in the training regime.

Despite ever-improving technology informing and driving problem solving and decision making, the appropriate supply of human capital remains hugely important, for the reasons spelt out above, so the resourcing of these people is critical. Introducing 'green' appointees into an IOC, with little or no prior operational experience is pointless, and although this may have occurred in past times, nowadays this is highly unlikely. Thus, the sourcing of appropriate individuals with suitable backgrounds is a priority. A census of Operations Controllers across IOCs would reveal that most staff generally have five or more years' experience in the role, though usually with vastly different backgrounds. Some, of course, have previous IOC experience gathered in another airline, perhaps a small regional carrier, or from another member airline within the group.

They may also have experience from an airline in another country, during which time they may or may not have served as junior officers as a common pathway into the Operations Controller role. Alternatively, or in addition, they may have gained some experience through other IOC roles (e.g., in crewing or flight-planning roles). This experience will serve them well for they will be attractive to the airline due to their high levels of understanding in terms of the types of problems, solutions and consequences thereof. They will also be well aware of the nature of problem solving within tight time-frames, and hence will have been subjected to the types of pressure common in this environment. Crucially, these individuals are also likely to recognise which stakeholders are, or need to be, involved in the process and the appropriate times for communicating information. In other words, they can 'hit the ground running'. Others may also have aviation experience, in co-related, operational areas of the industry such as having been a Pilot, Engineer, Air Traffic Controller or Flight Service Officer, or may have emanated from the military (especially the air force). Although not having had IOC experience per se, their backgrounds may nevertheless provide unique value to the airline. There is evidence, though, to suggest that thinking styles and the primary focus of attention are dominant according to the domain from which individuals emerge.[1] For example, staff recruited from an 'airport' environment (e.g., a ramp officer or terminal customer service role) are more likely to focus on airport-related issues, perhaps to the detriment of balancing the needs of the overall problem. A similar approach is likely with Pilots or Engineers, for example, or others from industry. While their knowledge, expertise and methods of operating in their former domains are fully acknowledged to contain valued skills, the IOC must be cognisant of any limitations that such recruitment presents.

Less common among Controllers is a background in allied industries such as logistics, or road or rail transport, such that the likeness of previous performance in comparable roles to the task required of Controllers is a prime argument for seeking such individuals. The commonality is very relevant and refers to the necessity for individuals to have had extensive operational exposure, particularly in similarly complex, high paced and intense environments, and with a focus on problem analysis and solving. One difference, though, may lie in a lack of exposure for considering the impact of disruptions on high volumes of customers, and with an increasing focus on customer journey management, this shortfall may be apparent. Occasionally, the net may be spread further to include other airline or even airport staff with ramp or terminal experience perhaps, or other aviation-related roles beyond operational functions including a number of commercial roles (e.g., Reservations) in the airline. The problem is that the further away from truly operational functions the greater the likelihood that the match between individual capability and requirements of the job at hand is diminished. This compares with a more traditional course of an apprenticeship served in supporting IOC roles such as a Crew Planner, which in that particular case, for example, would enable staff to become familiar with regulations and industrial awards pertaining to technical and cabin crews. Such a pathway has obvious advantages for grasping the concepts around disruption management.

KNOWLEDGE AND EDUCATION

The growing sophistication of the business of aviation calls for employees who have at least a working knowledge of the industry. Clearly, the greater the knowledge (ideally extending to an awareness of historical events), of regulatory and economic, operational, technical (especially relating to the performance of aircraft), commercial, and perhaps political aspects, the better the likelihood of understanding how the industry comes together to achieve the key aims of safety, legality and efficiency. More recently, airlines have begun to recognise the value of educational qualifications, particularly in the area of Aviation Management, which can provide individuals with a broad knowledge of industry and, subject to the course content, may even expose them to simulated problems not dissimilar to real events with comparable challenges and scope. Employment in the IOC has never really been subject to specific educational qualifications, but there is growing demand for advanced mathematical and computer literacy to provide for more sophisticated data analysis and systems support. Hence, some IOCs like to employ PhD qualified specialists, though in the day-to-day operations, there is no call for this level.

KEY ATTRIBUTES

Some of the key attributes vital for the operational control role have been categorised below to itemise relevant criteria. As has been described elsewhere, these attributes also apply to the role of Dispatcher (as defined earlier).

Motivation and passion

The role of Operations Controller calls for high levels of motivation. Individuals who are ideally suited to the task truly find their niche in such an operational setting. For the right people, there is a natural fit. As alluded to above, high achieving Controllers thrive in this environment, because the greater the complexity of the task in hand, and with their full immersion in a problem, the greater satisfaction they derive. They are results driven. If problem solving can be delineated in terms of degrees of solution outcomes, the following examples may help to distinguish perceived differences among Controllers. A *good* Controller might establish a workable solution to a problem that mitigates losses, recovers the schedule reasonably and uses resources sparingly. In decision theory, this approach is often called 'satisficing' – that is, achieving a solution that is satisfactory or 'good enough'.[2] It works, but that's all. In some events, this may be perfectly acceptable, given that time-frames may not permit further consultation or deliberation perhaps.

In contrast, though, an *outstanding* Controller will demonstrate skills well beyond this rudimentary level, expending considerably more effort to seek what, in their eyes, is an optimal or desirable solution. The attainment of such high goals comes about from a process of creating, testing and fine-tuning possible solutions, and being in a state of dissatisfaction until the best option is reached. To the uninitiated, observing an expert Controller's eyes seemingly 'jump' around the flight displays, or listening as a series of apparent disjointed questions are asked, would seem a most irrational manner to consider an event. Yet, the Controller will actually be creating a number of 'what-if' scenarios in his or her head and testing them for validity. This is how they sense whether potential solutions may or may not work. A key to this approach lies with the Controller's mastery of the situation, gained through stages of thorough preparation (e.g., during a briefing or handover stage), constant oversight, and an astute awareness of the potential consequences of any decision. This self-need for achievement is what gets their adrenalin flowing. It stimulates them, giving them a real 'buzz' as they seek to rectify adversity. To reach these heights they must be passionate about working in the operational environment and all that it brings in terms of challenges and opportunities to excel, and of course they have to be the right person for the job in the first place.

Disposition

The above section may appear as though these high achievers must be constantly stimulated at work and be excited sufficiently to produce the outcomes described above. Not at all. The reasons that high quality solutions are achieved don't emanate from a series of hectic responses, even in the midst of a chaotic disruption. Rather, they are due to the careful, deliberate approach that characterises the proficient Controller. There's no secret that at times, the IOC becomes quite chaotic. Routine problems in isolation are handled as a matter of course, but complex, multiple and ongoing situations test the resolve of all Controllers in time. One of the fundamental requirements of working as a Pilot or Air Traffic Controller is calmness under pressure, as decision making in these domains is critical, of course. The nature of the IOC in disruption mode (high pressure, noisy, many people, multiple events, conflicting objectives) calls for a similar approach, and needs individuals who are extremely resilient and determined, who can critique problems fully, and then construct carefully considered solutions. To do this implies not only an ability to multi-task, but an adeptness for juggling multiple problems, each with its own idiosyncrasies. They need to perform at their best in these conditions, so they need to exhibit a work ethic that meets this level.

Self-management and team-fit

At a personal level, individuals in this environment need to be in a sound state of health and condition. As shift workers with starting times variously at 0400, 1200, 1800 or 2300, for instance, and working anywhere between eight and 12 hours at a time, there must be a just recognition of the rigours of working around the clock and how this results in accumulated tiredness and fatigue, both at work and away from it. Similar to other roles in aviation operations, sufficient periods of quality rest are required for recovery. Staff rosters (should) play a key role in helping to mitigate the effects of fatigue, but individuals also need to take their own responsibility for maximising rest. One advantage usually enjoyed by shift workers in an operational environment is the knowledge that they can leave the workplace having endured a challenging and somewhat stressful shift, only to return the next day in totally different circumstances. Naturally, the inverse also occurs. But, the necessity to 'leave problems at work' for the oncoming shift to handle, is an important part of the mental and physical recovery process.

To conduct themselves calmly and professionally, yet still be determined to accomplish the task, individuals need a high level of self-control and behaviour. This includes the careful use of time management and, as discussed in later chapters, opportunities for some downtime as a means of escapism in the short term. Some of the tasks enable Controllers to work autonomously, carrying out a series of activities with otherwise little interaction. But the vast majority of work is team dependent, necessitating close cooperation with a mix of personalities, and tolerance for realising the team members' own goals and methods of working, while participating in and contributing to the overall objectives of the IOC. A Senior Controller needs to have well-honed leadership skills, capable of drawing others along throughout a disruption-management process, encouraging creativity, resourcefulness and persistence among the team members. This is vital to ensure the combined effort is directed appropriately.

COMMUNICATION SKILLS

A quintessential requirement of an Operations Controller is the ability not merely to communicate but to communicate extremely well! This necessitates the utmost care in listening, interpreting, liaising, negotiating, and informing of pertinent information about some aspect relating to the operation. It also demands a high level of understanding and the use of appropriate language and terminology. At times, the ability to articulate an argument strongly and clearly, or persuade others to realise and accept a point of view may also be crucial. The ability to communicate clearly 'at any level' is a cliché of course, but nevertheless highly relevant in this context. It translates to dealing with a diverse range of people such as team members, senior company management, airline Captains, Air Traffic Control, the country's regulator or a foreign government representative, for example. So, knowing what the information means, and to whom and when it needs to be communicated can be critical. As a result, language varies, as does communication technique and even emphasis as to the relevance or importance of a particular message.

The skills needed to adapt to these and other influences are therefore quite diverse to suit the circumstances. At times, the Controller needs to confront conflict between the players and may need to play the role of peace-keeper in some decision processes. At other times, knowing how and when to say 'no' may be necessary, as might sensing the need to escalate a communication more broadly or to a higher level. The nature of the communication then relies to an extent on the degree to which an individual must exercise empathy, while being fully aware of, and sensitive to, the interests and motivations of the other parties.

COGNITIVE SKILLS

A key part of the Operations Controller's (and indeed, Dispatcher's) task is to apply advanced thought processes in order to assess and solve complex problems in high-pressured, challenging circumstances. There are a couple of ways of considering approaches to decision making. One approach proposes that individuals follow a rational process.

Rational, deductive thinking

Rational thinking has been described as referring to 'a logical, step-by-step, systematic approach to decision making'.[3] Where such a step-by-step approach may be advantageous is for new Controllers who have little experience and thus, limited exposure to disruptions – especially complex disruptions. At a rudimentary level, they can follow a simple process (even writing down specifically numbered steps to help) to gain the appropriate information, talk to the right people, consider a number of options and select a preferred choice on which to act. This method may serve as a useful training tool to guide a new Controller through the decision process, as it may help them to consider all avenues in reaching the outcome. But in the case of most disruptions, of course, time to generate and analyse possible alternatives can be extremely limited. In addition, circumstances continually change, and information is often scarce, unreliable, confusing or contradictory. There are other limitations too. The individual may be narrowly focused on ensuring each step is followed to the detriment of focusing on the tasks themselves. The formal, perhaps written, steps cannot provide for every event, so a reliability gap also exists. Thus, the step-by-step approach may be suitable in some simple cases, but may not work in many others, resulting in doubt as to the legitimacy of the process. Where complex disruptions occur, not only is available time limited, but circumstances tend to change rapidly. Thus, information also changes rapidly and accumulates so fast that rationalising the volume of material to clarify the important and relevant messages may be too hard to do. A further argument is that the problems themselves are not necessarily well defined. This means that going through this sort of laborious process may not suit the circumstances of the typical operational challenge. This shortfall alludes to the use of an alternative approach to decision making. In this environment where problems are ill-structured, exhibit uncertainty and complexity and considerable time constraints, the use of intuition is usually more widespread.

Intuitive thinking – and thinking outside the box

Being intuitive is a personal trait that is, or at least should be, highly desired for membership of an IOC. It has been referred variously to having a 'hunch' or a 'gut-feeling',[4] or having a sense as to when something is likely to work or not. More experienced, Senior Controllers are usually highly intuitive. Naturally, they will be able to process the vagaries of a problem in a logical way. But what really sets them apart is an almost subconscious ability to cast beyond the obvious or known quantities, enabling them to perceive peculiarities – things that may appear evident on the surface, but somehow just don't look right. This ability to judge right from wrong, or the achievable from the unachievable, is a most valuable talent, such that whereas logic dictates they might act in a particular way, they sense other influences. For example, rather than following a number of steps normally taken (which may seem obvious to a less experienced Controller), they may instinctively wait, sensing something amiss or, perhaps, more opportune given the circumstances. This innate ability to distinguish between the discernible and the more obscure is one of the dominant features of intuitive thinking.

The expressions 'thinking outside the box' or 'outside the square' have been used on numerous occasions to highlight an ability to conceptualise problems and potential solutions by de-constraining the boundaries humans implicitly set. From an early age, humans are given parameters within which to think and act and are trained to operate accordingly, even to the extent of being penalised or dismissed should these limits be exceeded. So, as may be expected, potential solutions to problems are interpreted according to the level of experience and expertise of the Controller. A novice or raw Controller is likely to see the 'black and white' aspects of a problem and decide what may look to be a straightforward solution – for example, actioning a delay on a flight that, at face value, appears to be inevitable. In contrast, a more experienced and intuitive Controller may have some sense that the delay may not need to be implemented perhaps because of a potential change or other influence. In other words, this Controller realises that having too

COMPOSITION OF THE IOC

narrow a focus may only partially address a problem, and that part of the solution could emanate from an obscure or emerging source or may not as yet even be identified.

The sophistication of contemporary software packages (such as those driving and displayed by the Gantt chart) means that ready solutions to quite complex problems can sometimes be achieved with a number of keystrokes. This provides disruption recovery, for example, for aircraft and crew patterns and passenger journeys, among other features. Ironically, though, these tools may actually hinder the decision process in some circumstances. They will achieve a solution of sorts, which may be acceptable, and with the pressure of time may be the best option to invoke at that moment. But it may not be the *right* option, hence the need for and importance of human intervention. Extensive experience and especially intuition play a vital part in determining the merit of solutions suggested by disruption software in the IOC. For example, in a situation which is affecting a specific port (e.g., weather), part of the problem analysis stage may involve filtering the information on the Gantt display, so that only movements through that port are displayed. This limitation of visual information can reduce overall awareness. Perhaps part of the solution might have been to consider movements in close proximity to the port (overflying or operating through nearby ports). In this sense, the experienced, intuitive Controller shows a healthy respect for the software, but nevertheless is wary of the system-generated outcomes.

PROBLEM-SOLVING SKILLS

As could be expected, the main role in the IOC is problem solving. This is generally a reactive response to a situation. But part of the problem-solving process is having an unending awareness of what is happening across the network or particular section under watch.

Network monitoring

The need to monitor the flight schedules seems obvious, but other than gaining an initial awareness built from a shift handover or similar briefing, ongoing oversight is the principal means for maintaining full awareness of the operations. This is partly the reason that experienced Controllers exhibit a mastery of staying on top of events. Without disruption, monitoring is a case of observing departures and arrivals as they become updated. But, it is also a case of projecting well ahead of time to calculate implications of changing weather, for example, or other influences that may become disruptive. Mostly, though, disruptions in some form are common and frequent, so monitoring becomes more intense in determining potential sources of conflict and disharmony, requiring much of the Controllers' attention. This environment requires a continuous risk-management process. Assessing the validity of threats or potential disruptions is a matter of constant awareness and attention. For example, a relatively simple weather situation (e.g., strong crosswinds at a single-runway airport) immediately starts a chain reaction and in the Controller's mind, questions are raised such as – should the flight continue under present circumstances knowing that a diversion to an alternate destination is quite possible if the weather persists, or should a diversion be exercised now? If the flight were to divert, what is the consequence for the next (return or perhaps onward) flight, and are crew hours at risk? How can the passengers be accommodated (i.e., rescued) from a diversion port? So, the monitoring role is never really dormant. These sorts of mind games are at the forefront of the operation, no matter how small or seemingly insignificant an issue.

Problem identification and analysis

The occurrence of a disruption may be identified as a result of information received from a recognised source, or alternatively an *absence* of information from an otherwise reliable source. Then it is a matter for Controllers to identify the characteristics of the problem, determining its nature and potential threat to the schedules. Subject to the type of problem, ensuring that information is shared with associated IOC functions is important for a common understanding. For example, what may appear to be a straightforward, isolated delay to one flight in the eyes of a Controller may not create any disturbance for the aircraft pattern, but may well have significant consequences for the Crewing Department. So team coherence that shares and acts on common information is needed to correctly identify and explore all facets of potential and actual problems. This is fundamental to the integrity of the IOC structure. Once a problem is evident, an analysis stage involves a full determination of the extent of the problem. At this point, the Controller needs to validate the information received, in particular ensuring its source is credible and challenging any dubious message. Problem analysis will invite participation from other members of the IOC, so receptiveness to others' views and suggestions is vital to ensure analysis is as thorough as possible. The skills of the experienced Controller are evident in this stage, in terms of realising real and potential opportunities and identifying actions needed.

In other words, the analysis of a problem is more than simply contemplating what might happen in an event. The additional steps of generating and assessing options, each with its own projected outcomes and consequences, are also important and this is where the highly creative and intuitive minds lead to more advanced solutions.

Problem decision point and implementation

Key to the decision process is identifying points at which decisions need to be made. Too soon, and information may be incomplete, or other IOC functions may not have had sufficient input. Too late, and options may have vanished. It is a balancing act and is determined by a combination of factors underpinning the problem, the time available for optimising the solution and, crucially, the experience and expertise of the Controller. Notwithstanding the two decision-making styles outlined above, the Controller still has to ensure that sufficient information has been received and any likely change taken into account. Then, having consulted appropriately, and weighed all the options, the decision is enacted and outcome disseminated to all stakeholders, including customers. At times, the Controller needs conviction in his/her decision and the will to invoke the necessary choice as, with most decisions, there will be winners and losers. In a complex disruption, choosing the best option may be to the overall benefit of the airline but, in effect, compromises are often made resulting in penalising some aspects of the schedule.

ACQUIRING THE RIGHT PERSON

The appropriate recruitment, selection and training of Controllers is vital to the efficient and effective operation of the IOC. Yet, IOCs admit they have substantial difficulty finding and retaining the right resources. Appointees can be taught how to follow policies, operate systems, and be provided with training in leadership, communications and so forth. What is extremely difficult to do, though, is teach individuals how to be successful in disruption management. This is largely because of the innate qualities and traits needed for the role. So, finding the right person in the first place is essential.

RECRUITING AND SELECTING CONTROLLERS

The pool of potential applicants is varied depending upon the airline's approach. It really has a choice of external or internal sources.

Externally sourced

Should an IOC elect to source Controllers externally, the usual search would target existing Controllers serving other airlines, either domestically or internationally, or individuals working in associated roles and wishing to move into the IOC area. But the number of good, experienced Controllers worldwide (and wishing to relocate) is extremely limited. Very experienced, Senior Controllers and Dispatchers may be attracted to different conditions and remuneration, or the chance to expand their roles in a larger company or country. On the other hand, they may not be willing to leave their existing roles given personal circumstances. For this reason, sourcing this level of experience is increasingly difficult. Less senior Controllers, though, may be attracted. Notably, some of the pool may even fall outside industry. For example, a regionally based IOC had experienced great difficulty attracting suitably qualified candidates to their home town. To compensate, they found that recruiting candidates with a logistics industry (timber logging) background, albeit with little aviation knowledge, resulted in successful employment as the candidates could remain in the same region in which they had grown up rather than move to a city. The disadvantage of this approach was the nature of the foreign terminology, inexperience in communicating to a diverse group of stakeholders across the airline and adapting to the high-pressure environment of aviation life.

Ready sources of future personnel suitably qualified for IOC work are sometimes Pilots, Air Traffic Controllers or Flight Service Officers, who have elected to make a career change or whose careers may have been terminated due to medical conditions, for example. Their knowledge and expertise in their own areas is often invaluable for IOCs as they typically understand aviation rules, practices, procedures, terminology and factors affecting efficient operations. Most often, they have experienced the operational environment, its pressures and challenges, and are used to making rational decisions under pressure. Indeed they are methodical and risk averse. Therefore, they should have a mindset that supports the types of thought processes vital for an IOC environment, provided that they also possess the skills for 'out of the box' thinking as alluded to above. Other sources may include university students who have studied Aviation Management or similar degrees. With little or no exposure to the operational environment, their immediate value may lie more in supporting roles in the IOC, but nevertheless they may be identified at an early stage as promising for future roles, so a pathway leading eventually to IOC roles may be very attractive for the individual and a longer term viability for the airline. What students may bring also, are complementary skills such as analysis and research capability not generally found in IOCs, hence, as mentioned above, some instances of IOCs recruiting highly qualified (PhD) students, not for operational purposes but for sophisticated, exploratory systems and performance analysis.

Internally sourced

Should the IOC seek to employ internally, working through the airline's People Management (HR or Personnel) Department will usually bring the advantage of some ready knowledge of the employee and his or her past and existing roles and performance. In addition, employee records will inform the recruitment process more fully, and help to narrow the field somewhat. The focus of this search will usually concentrate on those already having had exposure to the operational side of the business, such as airport-related, customer handling, or planning and resourcing roles. In particular, a pathway into the IOC may already be in train through prior recruitment into, say, the Crewing areas, which has exposed the candidate to disruptions – especially crew disruptions – and taken into account the vagaries of the Pilot or Flight Attendant employment agreements and other legal requirements. This frequently proven pathway delivers an excellent grounding for operations roles. Sometimes airlines have a graduate trainee scheme in place which facilitates experience gained across a number of airline departments. On occasions, these may include IOC roles, albeit in junior positions. While the matching process may not immediately address the IOC's concern for the right person, the individual at least gains a worthwhile glimpse of the workings of the centre, even if only for three or six months.

Selection process

The process of selection is initiated typically by the People Management Department, who will narrow the field of candidates by culling the list and may conduct initial interviews themselves, with IOC management usually becoming involved once a short-list has been reached. Interviewing candidates facilitates a one-on-one opportunity to gauge a number of characteristics about an individual and establish basic information such as background, knowledge in the field, and prior experience. This can be enhanced by the inclusion of behaviour oriented questions that draw on past performance as a tool for forecasting future conduct. In addition, mock problems may be offered to elicit the candidate's thought processes and ability to articulate a reasoned and logical response, and may be far more beneficial than a rudimentary interview to explore the skill-set. The use of a simulation tool (mirroring elements of the actual system in use in the IOC) that provides a range of generated operational situations is a further means of delving more deeply into these thought processes. Coupled with a credible method for measuring performance against set benchmarks, this advanced tool can help to determine the way in which problems may be viewed and likely patterns of response – that is, identifying what may seem to come naturally, which is so hard to detect during a normal interview process. This sort of tool enables manipulation of weighted criteria case by case, so that highly desirable attributes can be explored with added rigour.

References and referees' checks

Reference checks that rely on written testimonials are rarely of much benefit as they are always written in a most positive light and fail to portray a true insight into an individual. By far, a preferred method is to select from a *referee* list and use a well-defined, explorative set of questions that encourages the referee to respond appropriately. Behavioural questions that seek to link past conduct with future performance are likely to yield reasonable results, provided that the questions are suitably modified to suit candidates' specific backgrounds, rather than a generic set, many of which can be irrelevant for the purpose. For example, asking a referee to describe *'Johnny's' personality* is of very limited value. But, relevant to someone's life skills (something that they could realistically have experienced) and pertinent to an IOC are more directed questions such as, 'When did you last see "Johnny" tackle a challenging problem? What did he actually do? How did he approach the problem? In what ways did he show initiative? How creative was he? How persistent was he in following it through to a conclusion?'

TRAINING CONTROLLERS

Training Controllers in an IOC takes many forms and may depend upon the Controllers' previous roles and levels of experience. Some, of course, will come to the airline with many years' involvement in operations and perhaps with some management experience, while others may be relatively inexperienced. Notwithstanding this, most training agendas commence with some form of induction training, which provides for a company overview, its structure, culture and norms, and company policies, and a more detailed operational rundown including structure and reporting lines, fleet characteristics, port information, airline practices and procedures, meteorology, operational systems, and so forth. However, for the Controller, the main thrust of training stems from learning on the job.

On the job

Often IOCs do not exhibit formalised training programs. Beyond the induction training, Controllers are typically introduced to the finer elements of the job, learning about normal and irregular operations, the factors that underpin each, and the subsequent management of them. A 'classroom' approach may be part of the initial training phase covering these and a lot of other information in considerable detail, perhaps over several weeks. But the transition of knowledge really comes to fruition in the practical, hands-on approach where the trainee is matched with an existing Controller, effectively mirroring their roster for a period. This 'buddy' method of training is arguably the most frequently used method in IOCs, enabling the Controller to learn from a mentor for several weeks. Provided the experienced Controller is an adept trainer (i.e. is motivated to impart knowledge and, importantly, specific techniques required for the task), and that the relationship between trainer and trainee is conducive, then some transfer of knowledge is likely, especially if the senior individual can elaborate sound cognitive processes. But there can also be disadvantages of buddy training. The method usually relies on learning the trade from one individual only, conveying that person's attitudes and habits (good and bad) to the trainee. This clearly relies on the interest and commitment of the mentor (i.e., a passionate and engaging approach versus one instructed to watch over and guide). A rotational method whereby the trainee accompanies several experienced Controllers over respective terms negates some of these concerns. Gradually the tasks are performed by the trainee with the mentoring Controller(s) guiding or observing only, as time ensues. Once 'signed off' the trainee is ready for a more permanent (but still junior) role. There is then a period of probation, during which time, both the airline and the individual need to assess the worth of the relationship. After all, a match only occurs when both parties establish a successful fit. Determining the value of a Controller is a process that usually takes at least 12 months and is also contingent on the level of exposure to a wide variety of complex situations and hence the degree of problem solving and decision making exercised.

Recurrent

Whereas initial training is vital to ensure trainees acquire sufficient knowledge and instruction to establish the fundamental tasks, recurrent training (e.g., annual, biennial) is often overlooked. Yet, recurrent training may be extremely beneficial, especially in airlines that are growing or changing considerably, or whose systems are becoming far more technologically capable. The focus of this sort of advanced training may lie in advanced problem solving or decision making or softer skill-based training in people management, negotiation, or leadership. More formalised courses will certainly provide considerable depth of information and in the case of regulatory body approved Airline Dispatch courses, offer a licence (where applicable) should this not already be an airline requirement.

FLIGHT DISPATCHER

The IOC employs Dispatchers to conduct key functions. In the US system, Flight Dispatchers are licensed airmen under FAA regulations and '[exercise] responsibility with the Pilot in Command in the operational control of a flight'.[5] Thus, legal responsibility for the conduct of a flight rests between the Captain (sometimes referred to as Commander) and the Dispatcher. Airlines in some non-US States subscribe to this system, either equipping their IOC with FAA licensed Dispatchers, or recognising their Dispatchers as holding a national dispatch licence within their own State jurisdiction, but not to the level of the FAA licence. Other States (e.g., Australia/New Zealand) do not require Dispatchers to hold a licence at all. For a more complete description of the Flight Dispatcher tasks and processes, see Kim (2018).[6]

ROLE

Whatever the regulatory basis, the tasks conducted within a dispatch function including flight planning, aircraft weight and balance, flight dispatch, and flight following (or monitoring), are assigned to the Dispatcher, whether that person is licensed or not, as indicated above. Whatever the system in use, the roles of the Dispatcher are instrumental within the IOC environment to inform and rectify problems concerning limitations due to aircraft performance, any other operational restrictions, or potential disruptions to schedule.

RESPONSIBILITIES

The responsibilities of the Dispatcher encompass many key aspects in relation to the airline's operations. First the role is responsible for the flight-planning process, that is the preparation and transmission of optimal, fuel-efficient plans taking into account efficient and expeditious planning of the route to be flown, extended twin engine operations (ETOPS) requirements, considerations for weather at any stage of the operation, equipment shortages or issues, airport conditions at departure, en-route and arrival ports, and any airspace problems such as airspace closures (e.g., due to military, resource issues, or political influence), or issues otherwise affecting flights. Second, the role is responsible for flight following whereby a monitoring process is employed to watch over each flight's progression, in particular noting, and advising of, any significant changes as a result of ATC requirements, or changes to weather conditions en route or at the destination, which may in turn alter the state of the fuel situation on board. This really implies a continuous risk-assessment process, constantly looking for signs of potential disruption to what may be an otherwise routine flight stage. Any changes to the above factors may require some form of intervention by the Dispatcher, requiring communication to one or more aircraft affected or likely to become affected, or to ATC, or airports, and then taking some form of positive action (such as instigating or concurring with a decision to divert a flight) as required.

KNOWLEDGE

A person involved in the Dispatch function needs excellent operational knowledge. This includes comprehensive knowledge of the regulatory framework within which the airline industry operates. It also requires thorough understanding of crucial sources of information such as the company's policies and procedures, sets of operating manuals (e.g., aircraft performance), methods for denoting operating limitations or variances (e.g., minimum equipment lists (MELs) and configuration deviation lists (CDLs)), crew contracts and agreements in place (e.g., a fatigue risk-management system (FRMS) for fatigue management), ATC rules and procedures, and so forth. In the US, the licensed Dispatcher must be fully cognisant of the pertinent Federal Aviation Regulations (FARs) governing the operation of flights. The aeronautical knowledge base extends to having an extensive familiarity and understanding of weather phenomena, and the various and numerous methods, protocols and symbolisms used in providing meteorological warnings and advice (e.g., SIGMETS, PIREPS, TAFORS – *see Table of Common Abbreviations*). In addition, knowledge and current awareness of any NOTAMs (notice to airmen) likely to impact airspace on the planned route, or airport facilities (such as, for example, runway length, airport works in progress, obstructions, change of tower hours), may be a source of concern, initiating discussions and actions similar to the previous description. Subject to the arrangements applying in the airline, the Dispatcher may also negotiate holding times, organise route clearances or permissions to operate, and arrange extensions of service, but these tasks may also fall under the control of the airline's staff at the airport.

SKILLS

Besides a mathematical and somewhat scientific mind to understand the principles involved in the task, the Dispatcher, similar to the Operations Controller, needs to demonstrate high levels of rational and intuitive thinking to manage processes appropriately and completely. The role calls for an excellent communicator at all levels across the industry, as at one moment liaison may be with an airport manager, the next negotiating with ATC, and then maybe having to brief and discuss possible offloads, fuel figures or diversion strategies with Senior Operating Captains. To do all this, the role also demands high-level interpersonal skills and an ability to handle pressure while openly displaying calmness and control. The ability to interact, negotiate, influence and at times accept advice from, other key functional areas of the IOC such as Meteorology, Maintenance, Load Control, Freight and Commercial areas, for example, is crucial.

MAINTENANCE WATCH

Maintenance Watch (or Control) is responsible for maintaining the serviceability of the airline's fleets throughout the network, by ensuring continuation of mechanical performance and reliability standards. Being located within the IOC provides for a primary interface between operational decision makers and maintenance expertise. The role requires high-level communication that may include liaising with maintenance resources around the network, as well as third-party contractors off-shore and airframe and engine manufacturers, for example. It may also require communication with a Captain while a flight is airborne in an attempt to trouble-shoot and ideally resolve an issue prior to the aircraft's arrival. In disruptions calling for maintenance intervention, the role may provide advice, seek other expert opinion, or deploy Engineers and/or parts to various locations to rectify an aircraft that has become unserviceable. Another focus is to monitor the status of maintenance equipment on board aircraft and at airports, and disseminate this information to key stakeholders. For example, the IOC usually contains a Maintenance status board displaying aircraft with deficiencies such as MELs, U/S APUs, or airports with unserviceable equipment (e.g., U/S GPU (ground power unit)) or other conditions (e.g., insufficient manpower to conduct planned work).

METEOROLOGY

Departments of Meteorology are usually government entities or agencies in most States. However, to augment the services provided by these authorities, many airlines employ qualified Meteorologists to provide a dedicated service. The role usually requires an individual with recognised expertise in meteorological science and extensive experience as an Aviation Forecaster in a meteorology office. In addition, there is a need for awareness and sound understanding of the legal framework and rules underpinning international aviation, procedures associated with airspace and navigation, and flight-planning theory and systems. The Meteorologist in an IOC is a valuable team member whose primary role is to monitor and analyse meteorological phenomena, provide operational briefings, advice and warnings, especially advising of any conditions (e.g., fog, thunderstorms and frontal activity, areas of turbulence, icing, and volcanic activity) that might impact the airline's operations, including conditions en route and those affecting origin, destination and alternate airport environments.

AIRCRAFT ALLOCATION/PLANNING

The role of the Aircraft Allocator/Planner provides a forward planning function within the IOC to ensure the operational fleet is legally and operationally prepared to undertake the flying program as determined by the commercial schedule. The role is proactive, generating a workable fleet plan that optimises aircraft usage in consideration of maintenance requirements and operational objectives.

Typically, the set of schedules received into the IOC prior to the day of operation does not take aircraft registrations (tail numbers) into account. So the actual task of allocating specific aircraft to each flight to create each flying pattern is part of the role of the Planner. The assignment of each aircraft is contingent on ensuring the aircraft capacity matches demand (predominantly a scheduling function, but once the schedule is handed over to the IOC, usually several weeks prior to the operating day, the planner can satisfy commercial requirements, manipulating the fleet by upgrading and downgrading aircraft types). Aircraft must also be operationally capable of performing the flying commitment, so selected aircraft may be identified in this process to ensure performance is optimised and any potential problem identified (e.g., payload offload). The aircraft assignment is also contingent on continued airworthiness (legal capability) requiring liaison with the Maintenance function to ensure all planned requirements and requests are met, or at least negotiated.

Load Control

Aircraft not only have both structural and volumetric limitations which affect the carriage of payload (passenger, bags, cargo, mail, etc.) and fuel, but the distribution of the load is critical for optimum aircraft performance as well as to enable efficient loading and unloading on the ground. As distinct from licensing or otherwise of Dispatchers, those who are responsible for the load planning and weight distribution of aircraft are indeed licensed whether these tasks fall within the Dispatcher's function or to a Load Controller (or Load Master). For more complete description of the role of a Load Controller, see Avery (2018).[7] In smaller airlines, the tasks may be combined into the role of one individual. Should any operating restriction or excess of weight result in an offload, the Load Controller liaises with the Dispatcher in the IOC so as to mitigate any effects well ahead of the flight departure time. From the flight plan, a provisional load sheet is produced, after which negotiation between the areas mentioned above reaches a desired load and balance situation, producing a final load sheet to be accepted and signed off by the Operating Captain. The Load Control Centre is usually a centralised function, for reasons of efficiency. Load Controllers are typically licensed (i.e., endorsed) to provide load advice for multi-types of aircraft. If the airline itself does not conduct its own Load Control, the role often outsourced, usually due to cost, either to another airline, or to a specialist organisation which could be located anywhere in the world.

CREW CONTROL

The Crewing function (including various titles/roles such as current day control, rostering, resourcing, planning, and support) deals with managing the day-to-day flying commitments of the airline's crews. There are two separate functional areas within the IOC (i.e., Flight, Technical or Pilot Crewing, and Flight Attendant or Cabin Attendant Crewing). The main purpose for including representatives from both Crewing areas in the IOC is to provide timely and appropriate decisions concerning crew availability and deployment in the face of disruptions. To do this, they need detailed knowledge and expertise to interpret and apply rules according to the international and State regulations, specific crew industrial agreements and the airline's FRMS in place at any time. These agreements differ for Flight Crews and Flight Attendants, are complex and far reaching, and so important that misinterpretation may result in illegal assignments or in costly remedies for the airline. Thus, a sound knowledge of regulations, crewing contracts or other agreements between the airline and crews is needed, as is a knowledge of policies concerning safety and well-being of crews. The maintaining of extensive and concise records (e.g., duty hours, rest breaks, maximum duty over various time-frames) is a regulatory and industrial necessity, so attention to detail and persistence in attaining high-level outcomes are vital in the role. Working in the IOC's pressured environment naturally calls for proven analytical and problem-solving skills, so individuals responsible for Crewing functions need to be highly motivated and dedicated to achieving targets. Besides the current day control, additional crew areas such as those responsible for formulating pairings and rosters and for providing supporting roles are normally located away from the central decision makers.

COMMERCIAL AND CUSTOMER JOURNEY MANAGEMENT

The focus of the Commercial function is of course customers. But, capacity adjustments may be required prior to the day of operation (within the IOC window of, say, 2–7 days), perhaps as a result of a previous disruptive situation, or some special request for additional capacity (e.g., sudden increase of demand on a route). So, capacity adjustments may be occurring right up to the operating day, as the schedule is fine-tuned to maximise opportunities. Of course, a large part of the role entails disruption management and the commercial activities necessary to protect customers.

The CJM role has become of increasing importance as noted several times earlier. The inclusion of this key role in the IOC is to ensure operational decision making takes into account any commercial factors affecting the process, such that the impact on customers is realised and minimised. It is the commercial 'voice', or customer advocacy within the IOC, and its influence contributes to identifying appropriate avenues of disruption management, such as, for instance, nominating which flights should, or should not, be targeted for delay or cancellation. Key areas of focus include contributions to IOC decision making in terms of proposing least impact flights to disrupt or development of recovery plans for disrupted passengers, identification of VIP and CIP customers and protection thereof in the event of journey disruption.

Increasingly the function plays an important role in pre-empting or minimising disruptive effects to customers, but when these occur, the role takes into account commercial decisions (with budgetary implications) such as the need for providing re-bookings on alternative flights (or airlines – whether allied to the original airline or not), accommodation, transport, meals and customer compensation. These decisions are the result of significant communication and liaison with the relevant parties such as airlines, airport staff, reservations, hotels and so forth. With most airlines having sophisticated loyalty programs, the need for recognition and appropriate treatment of high tiered customers forms part of the emphasis of the recovery process. Knowledge of Customer, Inventory and Reservations systems is, of course, critical to the role, but equally important is the skill-set for analysing situations and finding solutions in the customers' best interests but also in a commercially responsible manner. The individuals in these roles must be extremely customer service focused and able to communicate and engage across a diverse customer base. Like other roles in the IOC, they must be passionate for their work.

ATC FLOW CONTROL/SLOT CONTROL

In many airports, the management of air traffic is subject to the use of Air Traffic Flow Management (ATFM), which seeks to optimise the use of airspace in and around airports, as well as providing a system that is consistently applied and is fair to the airlines wishing to use the airport. The role of an airline Slot Controller (or in the case of the USA, perhaps a specially classified Dispatcher tasked as an ATC Coordinator, or similar titled role) is to liaise with the Air Service Provider in order to negotiate arrival and departure slots for the airline. With limited slots available, and airline disruptions occurring that alter departure and arrival timings, part of the role of Slot Controller is also liaising with other users of the system (other airlines) with a view to swapping slots between them, to suit all parties. With ever increasing traffic volumes and congestion problems at many airports, the role plays a fundamental part in the IOC. But when disruptions deteriorate considerably, the Slot Controller becomes a key person, as much of the recovery process may hinge upon successfully achieving accessible slot times.

AIRPORTS COORDINATOR

Some IOCs have an Airports Coordinator or liaison representative. This position serves as a contact point between the IOC and the Station Managers (or Port Coordinators), thus providing direct two-way communication and, importantly, a channel for directing information and decisions affecting that port. These port functions are the eyes and ears of the IOC and are vital cogs in the operational environment. The relationships among the airport staff and the IOC representation clearly need a high level of interdependence and cooperation, remembering that in times of disruption, each airport will be vying to secure its own recovery and won't have the overall network tolerance needed to balance the airline's operation. Thus, the role as airport spokesperson within the IOC needs to argue each case on its merits, while at the same time being well aware of the overall impact and the need for everything to knit together. This requires individuals with an in-depth knowledge of the ways in which the various airports function, including the subtleties of ownership and control, and the internal and external pressures upon them to perform. They need to be well aware of the tools used for measuring airport performance, such as a Precision Timing Schedule whereby each process and task (e.g., baggage unloading, fuelling, catering) has a specific time moment and duration during the turnaround time of an aircraft. Importantly, they also need to acknowledge the nature of the critical relationship between the airport and the airline customer.

FREIGHT LIAISON

Having freight representation within the IOC is another vital cog in the operational wheel. The freight function has oversight into what is loaded 'below the wing'. Maximising payload on every flight includes maximising the freight uplift where possible, and the airline company in partnership with freight agencies need to avoid lost opportunities for freight carriage. During the final trim of the aircraft they are constantly liaising with Flight Planning and Load Control to maximise the cargo space when weight is paramount to the operations, as is the case in ultra-long-haul flights. In these more critical operations, it is highly desirable to accommodate at least the *premium* freight.

There are a number of reasons why freight uplifts are so important to the IOC. For example, the airline may have leased out cargo space to a large freight or mail organisation and honouring those contractual agreements is a high priority. There may be carriage of live animals, perhaps as transfers between zoos or other organisations or in association with a worldwide breeding program, for example. There may be a need for live human organ transfers requiring precise coordination and especially an awareness of environmental conditions both on board the aircraft and at airports being served. On some occasions, there is a need for repatriating human remains, requiring a high level of coordination and organisation, and of course a degree of compassion. In certain cases, some countries may also require a military escort to accompany the remains with particular attention given during an aircraft transfer.

The freight representative(s) is responsible for liaising with external and internal sources such as suppliers to ensure consignments are carried correctly and to enable any special needs, and engineering to ensure the aircraft hold capability and serviceability are suitable and methods for securing items are appropriate. A key role for freight representatives in the IOC is their ability to ensure a high level of customer focus. In the event of a sizeable delay, for example, they are able to contact a shipper of perishable items such as fresh flowers or seafood for a particular market prior to the perishables leaving the cool rooms, thus enabling maximum product life and freshness as far as possible.

SOCIAL MEDIA

The presence of a social media section in the IOC has become one of significance. Social media monitoring can be a powerful tool. In some instances, the social media function may provide the first indication of an issue that could impact a departure – even one occurring outside an airport environment (e.g., a transport stoppage or accident may hinder or prevent customers arriving at an airport. Airport staff may not be aware at all, but social media platforms may have prior information). In terms of any perceived threat event (e.g., political or social unrest) posted on any social media platform, they may also have a role to play in helping to track electronic footprints. So they can serve as a main point of contact, both inwards and outwards in relation to customer-related events and communications related to airline issues such as disruption management and recovery, systems issues, and incidents, for example. They have the ability to assist business areas of the airline, especially where external contact is needed, through a number of means including telephone, web chat, SMS, and email.

SECURITY

If the IOC has security representation, the main focus is to provide an immediate point of reference and response for security issues occurring within or external to the airline. The role monitors worldwide security events and provides information and advice should threats be identified that are likely to affect the airline, its staff, customers or facilities. With membership of the IOC comes affiliation and a close working relationship with other key areas. So events that arise through social media with security implications, for example, can be assessed rapidly. Similarly, social media can also be used as a means of informing stakeholders of security events.

EXTENDED COMMUNICATIONS

The larger the airline, the greater the need for a sophisticated central Operations Control system. Beyond the internal relationships are numerous other key associations – some as extensions of the internal functions such as crew rostering, resourcing and support. These groups have little direct impact on the operating day but belong to the same functional area as the Crewing representatives in the IOC who have the decision autonomy. A similar approach is valid for Engineering/ Maintenance and Commercial functions. Only a small, but key representation (e.g., Maintenance Control or Watch, or Commercial/CJM) resides in the IOC but, as expected, vast Engineering and Commercial resources exist within the airline.

Airlines that have formed considerable main port or 'hub' activities, also need a suitable structure to manage those ports, as operational activity in such large centres demands considerable oversight. Port staff are obviously well placed to deal with local cultural issues, and of course will have multilingual capability. In the larger ports – especially those that serve as airline hubs, control of these activities may be performed by a hub control centre, and may be managed by a Hub Controller and team, whereas management of smaller ports is usually under the organisation of a Station Manager, Port Coordinator, Ground Operations Coordinator, Apron Movements Coordinator, or similar title. Due to the size of international hub airports, the activities within the hub are, in a sense, pivotal operations centres in their own right. Hence, they have a degree of authority for managing the airline's operational performance through the hubs. The distinction between the hub control and the IOC is clear though; the hub manages the activities of the port and all its own issues, and acts as a filter for the IOC, while the IOC manages the broader network. Hence, the roles of the hub control do not lie within the jurisdiction of the IOC, but nevertheless there must be a very close affiliation between both parties, as the hub or port operation are the eyes of the IOC at those ports. Thus, the relationship needs to be very strong and trustworthy.

EXTERNAL RELATIONSHIPS

There are also several non-airline external affiliations of importance to the IOC. Various arms of government may need to be consulted (e.g., national government covering operations within the State, and national and foreign governments covering operations for flag (international) carriers). This may be necessary in relation to requests for curfew dispensation, search and rescue flights, or charter flights or similar reasons. Figure 2.2 presents the structure of these external relationships described above.

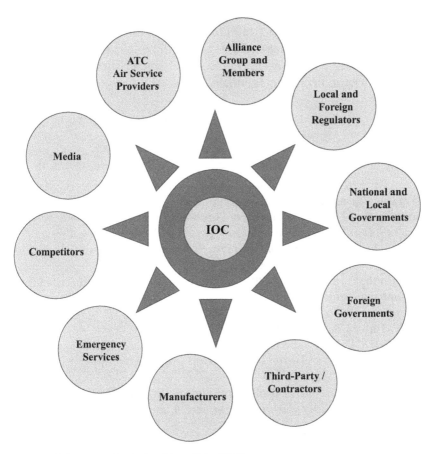

Figure 2.2 External relationships of the IOC

Key Challenges for IOC Management

With the mounting pressure on airlines to perform successfully in an increasingly challenging and more complex environment, the IOC becomes even more integral in the management of day-to-day operations. Software will continue to develop and provide more effective ways to streamline processes and accomplish tasks. But there must always be the aspect of human intervention as a necessary mediator in managing the operation. Attention to finding, grooming, developing and retaining the elite levels of talented individuals with highly advanced decision making and problem-solving capabilities, among others, must be seen as fundamental to the future IOC. Human investment and development are central to retention strategies, and sustained performance to deliver required outcomes depends, to a considerable extent, on a blend of attracting the right skill-sets and personal characteristics and applying appropriately focused training agendas.

Notes

1 Bruce, P.J. 2011. *Understanding Decision-making Processes in Airline Operations Control*, Farnham, Ashgate, p. 156.
2 Simon, H.A. 1976. *Administrative Behavior: A study of decision-making process in administrative organizations* (4th ed.), New York, Free Press.
3 Bruce, P.J. 2011. *Understanding Decision-making Processes in Airline Operations Control*, Farnham, Ashgate, p. 15.
4 Sadler-Smith, E., and Shefy, E. (2004). The intuitive executive: Understanding and applying 'gut feel' in decision-making. *Academy of Management Executive, 18*(4), 76–91.
5 FAR FC Part 65 Subpart C S65.51(a).
6 Kim, G. 2018. Dispatch and flight following, in P.J. Bruce, Y. Gao and J.M.C. King (eds) *Airline Operations: A practical guide*, Abingdon, Routledge, pp. 239–253.
7 Avery, P. 2018. Aircraft load planning and control, in P.J. Bruce, Y. Gao and J.M.C. King (eds) *Airline Operations: A practical guide*, Abingdon, Routledge, 220–238.

3 OPERATIONAL PLANNING AND PREPARATION

INTRODUCTION

With some understanding of the nature of an IOC, this chapter considers the extensiveness of planning and preparatory stages prior to the day of operation. For the IOC to achieve its objectives, sections engaged with pre-operational functions need to get a lot right. Subject to the specific function, preparatory stages may imply time-frames of many years in advance, as in the case, for example, of the airline's choice of business and network model, development of route and port selection, and selection and acquisition of aircraft. With these all in place, of course, shorter time-frames apply to many other functions as the operating day looms. This chapter explains the business, commercial and operational factors that determine the direction and ways in which airlines prepare for the operating day.

Business Factors

BUSINESS MODEL

The business model adopted by airlines plays a significant part in the manner in which airlines develop their network and their operating philosophy. Besides the obvious commercial and marketing needs, determining the desired model will have implications for schedule generation, aircraft equipment selection, service levels, contractual arrangements with third parties, especially for ground resources, and so forth. Adopting a modus operandi of continuous improvement, the focus of senior management is on external factors such as regulatory requirements, changes to competition, alliances and partnerships, ownership arrangements, and industry opportunities and threats, and internal factors such as cost control, productivity, and the need to meet operational and commercial objectives, for example. Differences between (generically termed) legacy or full fare carriers, and low-cost carriers determine the methods by which the airline will address these factors.

Network design: hub and spoke vs point-to-point

A hub and spoke network design is typified by a central airport (hub), or a number of key hubs if the airline is of considerable size, through which passenger traffic is distributed often to several other destination ports (spokes). This type of network design facilitates intense waves or banks of flights[1] several times a day, which generates considerable activity at the hub airports during these occurrences. The principle underlying this level of activity is the extensive levels of connectivity for passengers with the aim of a carrier fully retaining the travel itineraries through the customer journey. In contrast, a point-to-point model emphasises individual markets[2] such that customers can fly directly from one airport to another airport, so long as the airline provides such a direct operation.

The hub and spoke design adopted by an airline at its creation (or re-creation) determines the types of schedules that are produced to enable the banks to function as efficiently as possible and, as a consequence, the aircraft types needed to service each market. For instance, an international or large domestic hub and spoke carrier will typically operate wide-bodied aircraft as the spokes generate considerable traffic not only to and from the hub per se, but also with each other, due to the high degree of connectivity that defines the model. Point-to-point carriers operate over less dense routes as demand is more representative of the traffic serving the origin and destination only. Hence, aircraft choice usually (but not always) focuses on narrow-bodied types.

Each of these models characterises the ways in which an IOC needs to manage disruptions. Resolving problems that occur with several large aircraft (having numerous crew numbers), with high payload in comparison with more frequent but smaller aircraft with lower payloads requires quite different strategies and solutions. Airlines operating with a hub and spoke model may become highly exposed with the occurrence of severe disruptions to the major hubs, as a significant proportion of their networks may be affected. In contrast, point-to-point operators may be able to isolate operational problems to specific routes or geographical regions, and thus limit greater network disruption. These strategies are explained more fully in Part II of the text.

OPERATING ROUTES/LICENCES

Aircraft operating across international boundaries must hold a route licence permitting the operation. The airline's Scheduling Department, or an offshoot, will normally have arranged in advance for all appropriate licences, overflight clearances, arrival and departure slot times or any other legalities related to the network's schedules. On the current day, any variances, say due to a diversion or requirement for additional clearances will be micro-managed by the IOC itself.

OPERATING PORTS

The decision to select operating ports is part of an airline's commercial strategy and culminates as a result of months or even years of direction, opportunity, and negotiation. Although driven by commercial interest, operational input (e.g., from flight operations, performance engineering, the airline's own airport representation, and numerous others) informs the process to ensure the port and route structure are appropriate and that the airline has the suitable facilities (e.g., airport infrastructure such as appropriate navigational aids, sufficient runway, taxiway and hard stand apron areas, and terminal conditions including customer check-in capability to match proposed schedules, customer premium lounges, gate lounges served by aerobridge and/or remote parking, sufficient fuel capability, hangars, and so forth), legal arrangements and appropriate resources in place.

Port readiness

Closer to the operating day, port readiness is essential to ensure scheduled services can be accommodated on the ground, in terms of sufficient parking spaces, use of contracted ground-handling facilities, equipment and service delivery, engineering support, terminal check-in on the day, and provision and allocation of appropriate gates. Either the airport authority or the airline's airport staff will be responsible for gate allocation. This is an important planning task to ensure that gates are used efficiently, congestion is minimised, and the schedule can be achieved without delays to inbound or outbound flights. Part of the process of efficient port operations also calls for parking connecting flights within reasonable distances of each other to facilitate passenger convenience, and in the case of many short-haul or domestic operations, crew convenience, as they too may need to change aircraft.

FLEET SELECTION AND MIX

Fleet planning, selection and acquisition is a long-term corporate strategy, dependent on the direction set out in its strategic planning and business model. There is typically a long lead time to acquire aircraft, especially if receiving a new aircraft from a manufacturer, or having acquired one from another airline or leasing company perhaps, all of which typically spend some time with Engineering, prior to entry into service. In the case of the first of a new model of aircraft introduced into the airline, this may not be released for line flying until several weeks after arrival, perhaps having conducted 'showcase visits' to various ports. Although not in commercial service, their operation will still fall under the monitoring and control of the IOC.

Determining the number and type of aircraft to be acquired is driven by a mixture of commercial need and financial capability. Some fleets will be boosted by additional units of the same model, having little impact on integration into existing operations. On the other hand, integrating new aircraft types into the existing fleet inevitably results in some hybrid mix that can be difficult to manage on a day-to-day basis. From an IOC perspective, aircraft entering the fleet need to be mission capable as soon as they are released by Engineering for line service.

COMMERCIAL FACTORS

THE COMMERCIAL SCHEDULE

Airlines plan their operations years ahead of the current day. From a determination of the cities to be served, network design and desired route structure, and following a long, exhaustive process to ensure all relevant considerations have been taken into account, a flight schedule will emerge. Commonly, airlines will produce a major timetable according to summer and winter periods. This is largely due to significant changes in seasonal weather, and holiday period durations, particularly in the northern hemisphere, leading to significant changes in demand for travel. Thus, the process will be a function of the regulatory framework, market demands, required aircraft mix with any operational performance and limitations, resources and manpower, and competition.[3] At first, the schedule will be an ill-defined set of flights that, over many months, will be manipulated and modified to meet more exacting commercial targets within a multitude of constraints and limitations. Similarly, the operational aspects are also planned in significant detail, right up to the evening prior to the day of operation. Hence, operational preparedness is essential to optimising the day's operation as planned. In the count-down to the day of operations, there are numerous challenges to be faced, due to competing demands primarily from the airline's own commercial and engineering activity, but also from outside demands such as ATC or airport gate resources. Considerations within the many functional areas of the IOC must take into account demands for resources that may be based, for example, on contractual arrangements (e.g., Pilots, Flight Attendants, Engineers).

The Schedules Planning (Scheduling) Department's task is to build, develop and then fine-tune the flight schedules to the point of maximum utility. This translates to having met all legal and regulatory limitations, corporate and commercial objectives (such as achieving target load factors and target market share), and realising optimal efficiency regarding use of resources, all with the utmost in customer focus at the forefront. At the point of handover from the Scheduling Department to the IOC, all these objectives and more should be met. The extensive build-up of the schedule will also have incorporated the ideal utilisation of Pilot and Flight Attendant crews, taken into account available resources with inbuilt capacity to cover contingencies, met any maintenance requirements for servicing, repair, or other considerations, considered any airport and airspace restrictions, and so forth.

FLEET UTILISATION

Part of the task of building a schedule is programming flights to meet the commercial objectives such as capacity required for a city-pair (route), frequency and timing of flights, and provision of connection times to enable travel across the network. The schedule that is produced is manifested in terms of an operational utilisation of aircraft, displaying sequences of flights in a chronological order of operating time. So, operating patterns of flights emerge which may all fit essentially within one day for a domestic schedule, or span across several days for a flag (international) carrier. These patterns of flights are initially assigned to an aircraft *type*, rather than an individual aircraft registration or tail number; a process that occurs much closer to the actual day of operation. Building up these patterns takes into account the requirements for matching demand across each city-pair or route, with capacity (right aircraft on the right route). Of course, Scheduling must be cognisant of the capabilities of the chosen aircraft type, as the aircraft must be able to operate the route structure with the right performance characteristics to carry the required payload. This is a very iterative process, continuously evolving and changing.

As demand fluctuates, the capacity-matching process needs to adapt, with the result that the schedule build-up process is in a very fluid state for a long time. In addition, changes to *types* of aircraft being matched against demand call for changes to the crew allocations and patterns (especially pilots), further complicating the process. A third player; the Engineering or Maintenance Department, also plays a key role, as planned maintenance work needs to be considered in the schedule-building process to ensure the fleet remains capable of meeting the operating requirements. In larger fleets, it is common for a number of aircraft to be excluded from the composition of the schedule, to allow for rotating several airframes through heavy maintenance. Where possible, the maximum number of aircraft are programmed to be available to meet peak travel demands such as major events and holiday periods. In some fleets, though, where all fleet units are committed to flying patterns, or in the case of smaller airlines with low fleet numbers, this may be less feasible.

Commercial and operational nexus

It can be appreciated from the above points, that the nexus between the Commercial Scheduling Department, and the operational areas, predominantly Operations Control, Crewing (both Pilot and Flight Attendants) and Engineering Departments is challenged at times due to the differing philosophies underpinning their functions. To reach commercial objectives, schedules may be designed in such a way that results in operational inefficiencies or exposes the future operation to weakness in the face of disruption. For example, if a number of 'tight' schedules requires precise crewing connections between a number of flights, with little alternative crewing solution, such that a delay to a key flight may compromise these connections, the consequential effects could be widespread, with little room for effecting a fitting recovery. So, the schedule-build process needs involvement from all stakeholders, whose specific interests and concerns need to be considered thoroughly, as alienating any part of this relationship will lead to suboptimal outcomes.

Schedule robustness

Robustness refers to the ability of a schedule to withstand disruptive shocks during a day of operation. Schedules are built according to commercial demand that results in a series of programmed flights ideally having an optimum yield of passengers and meeting commercial targets such as desired load factors and market shares. Hence, flight timings where possible, and depending on the business model operated by the airline, may be tuned to customer preferences, such as satisfying peak demands (e.g., morning or afternoon business), providing attractive departure and arrival times, and suitable levels of frequency. From an operational point of view, there are a number of subtle ways schedules can be fine-tuned to add robustness and help the IOC manage on the day of operation. For example, extending the total schedule time (departure to arrival) can help to alleviate ground-holding times at busy airports, and scheduling additional ground time *between* flights (called buffering) can assist in recovery from late-running flights.

Schedule flexibility

Besides meeting the constraints above, robustness should also take into account opportunities for swapping aircraft of the same type (like for like), enabling greater flexibility in day-to-day operations. This degree of flexibility may also satisfy requests by Crewing to facilitate crew connections between flights, or by Engineering for particular aircraft registrations (tails) to be committed to particular patterns or to particular ports for maintenance work. Further, flexibility may enable better efficiencies in gate allocation in major ports. Sometimes, the schedule build results in lengthy dwell times at airports (e.g., a turnaround time of 5, 12 or longer, hours). The volume of traffic expected to use the parking gates at some airports often requires aircraft to be towed off-line and parked remotely until the next scheduled commitment. This time is also used on occasions for maintenance work. Depending on the configuration of the airport facilities, towing times may be implicated in delaying outbound flights.

OPERATIONAL FACTORS

AIR NAVIGATION

Airlines are continuously striving for greater economy and efficiency in the way in which business is done. Advances in technology within Air Navigation Service Providers (ANSPs) and in the various ground and satellite navigation systems have improved navigation procedures enabling, for example, reductions in vertical separation, continuous descents into airports (rather than step descents), sophisticated means of flight tracking (such as 'flextracks'), performance-based navigation, and enhanced systems of air traffic flow. Capitalising on these technologies, properly equipped aircraft and trained crews are increasingly able to optimise their flight paths, leading to savings in time and fuel burn. Each of these deserves considerable discussion elsewhere, but the point here is that the growing use of these evolving procedures and systems has beneficial effects on the operation of the airline and therefore is of great interest for IOCs.

AIRSPACE

In many countries, airspace is divided into areas determining civil and military use. Regular public transport (RPT) operations are usually unable to traverse military areas or may need special clearances to do so. In time of conflict, restrictions are often in place either limiting or preventing the overflight of dangerous regions. The effects of restrictions such as these are pronounced for airlines. Flight planning around areas of potential or current conflict is necessary, with the result that additional flight time, extra fuel burn and extended crew duty hours will add to the cost of the operation, and also extend the arrival time at the destination with consequential connection and turnaround time considerations. In some severe cases, flights may need to be cancelled until the conflict is resolved or is deemed safe. Another consequence may derive from recurrent late arrivals at a destination. If the particular destination airport operates to a slot system (which applies to most major airports now), and a scheduled flight continually fails to meet the scheduled arrival slot above an allowed percentage margin, the slot time may be taken away from the airline. In the case of losing Grandfather rights, for example, such a loss would be devastating for an airline. A threat such as this is likely to prompt the IOC into investigating solutions to prevent multiple occurrences.

CURFEWS

Many airports around the world have legislated curfews in place. These are artificial limitations, in response to community, pressure group and environmental concerns surrounding noise and other pollutants. Curfews relate to RPT operations, and generally not to military, medical or emergency flights. Typically, curfews apply to jet aircraft above a certain gross weight (e.g., 34,000 kg/75,000 lb), whereas other 'low noise' aircraft (e.g., some approved jets, smaller jets and turboprops) are able to operate during curfew hours, but often are subject to capped movement numbers.

There may be further concessions for particular flights (e.g., international) which operate under a 'Grandfather' clause (i.e., long-established rules continuing to be applied), meaning that some flights (large aircraft) may operate within the curfew period. Curfews predominantly operate from 2300–0600, but the exact times may vary according to local conditions and arrangements. Under a Grandfather clause, some airports may allow a number of landings (but generally not take-offs) between 2300–2359 and 0500–0600 (often termed shoulder periods), or some other variation or combination. In terms of operating aircraft to suit curfew restrictions, a whole set of rules typically applies to the precise times that an aircraft needs to request and be given pushback, taxi and/ or take-off clearance, or is required to become airborne and cross the airport fence, prior to the commencement of the curfew period. Further, the direction of the duty runway may also be restrictive for take-offs and/or landings, due to the incidence of noise over nearby community areas. So, if a nominated runway is not suitable due to wind or other conditions, operations may not be permitted.

There is usually a system of monetary fines for curfew breaches and despite this, an airline may occasionally elect to depart late and pay the fine (provided they have ATC clearance to operate, of course). The rationale is that should a late-night take-off not occur, the cost and disruptive effects of cancelling the service with the resultant wait for the crew to take crew rest, likely hotel accommodation, shortage of an aircraft in the network, missed connections at the destination, and any other consequential flow-on, may be well in excess of the fine. There may be a system of dispensation available, whereby in an extenuating circumstance, such as the occurrence of a wide-ranging and unpredicted disruption (major weather event) leading up to a significant holiday period (e.g., major religious events), the commencement of curfew may be relaxed by, say, 30 minutes. This type of dispensation is most likely to rely on a government departmental approval system but may in extreme cases require a higher level of government sanction. Other than curfew restrictions, there may also be limitations as to the availability of control tower staff, such that the tower (and therefore ability to authorise landings or take-offs) is only available at particular times. In some dual civil/military airports, ATC services are provided by the military, thereby governing operational hours.

SLOTS

With ever increasing demand in air travel, most airports around the world are slot constrained. The International Air Transport Association (IATA) categorise airports in terms of congestion, applying a system with Levels 1, 2 or 3, depending upon a number of factors such as capacity of the airport infrastructure (runways, taxiways, gates, etc.) or government-imposed conditions, either of which limits the airport's capability to meet traffic demand.[4] The process of slot allocation requires airlines to have a slot allocated by a coordinator in order to arrive and depart at the airport when slot allocation is active. Not only may the creation of schedules be governed by slot allocations, but day-to-day operations may also be affected by normal and non-normal influences. The IOC matches the COBT or EOBT (calculated or estimated off-blocks time) with slot allocation to ensure any discrepancy does not exceed a permitted allowance (e.g., plus 15 minutes or minus 5 minutes), aware that non-compliance may result in some penalty – typically additional airborne holding time. If otherwise delayed flights miss their allocated slot times, then renegotiation of the slot(s) if this is possible, or having to await the next available slot, may result in considerable disruption to the network. Should an arrival slot be extended, the flight may then be subject to further flight time, implying additional fuel burn, increased crew hours, and potential threat to onward connections and aircraft turnaround time at the destination. Of course, gate parking, ground resources, and reduced turnaround time of the aircraft may also be consequential effects.

NOISE ABATEMENT

Procedures determining the departure or arrival tracks of aircraft are used to mitigate the effects of noise over sensitive residential or other community areas. These procedures provide for adherence to specific flight paths and power settings, with nominated heights for manoeuvres such as circling, or conducting approaches into, or departures out of, an airport. They also provide for using nominated or preferred runways (e.g., utilising a specific runway for arriving and departing aircraft), and the use or limitation of applying reverse thrust on arrival, especially for operations conducted inside the curfew period (with due dispensation).

AIRPORT CHARACTERISTICS

Airports vary enormously in terms of their geographical location, altitude, environmental surrounds, physical layout, numbers and configuration of runways and taxiways, apron design, parking facilities, fuelling points, and other passenger and freight areas. Some of these characteristics result in considerable performance limitations affecting aircraft taking off. For example, the high-density altitude of Denver International Airport, USA (5,400 ft above sea level) can limit aircraft take-off performance, which may reduce the uplift of payload or fuel, despite the airport's very long runways. In the centre of Australia, Alice Springs experiences very high temperatures during the Australian summer-time (e.g., 40+ degrees Celsius), resulting in significant payload limitations, or sometimes the need for a technical stop to uplift fuel. Other airports may be located in a valley, on a plateau or side of a hill with subsequent restrictions in operating in or out. Locations such as these are often characterised by difficult weather conditions (e.g., cross-winds, turbulence, wind shear) which may affect aircraft approaches and landings in particular. Other airports (such as Queenstown in New Zealand, Juneau in Alaska) may be surrounded by terrain features that necessitate very precise navigational approaches (e.g., RNP), for which aircraft must have suitable navigational equipment and pilots who are specifically trained.

PAVEMENT CONCESSIONS

Some airports have pavement strength limitations with regard to the maximum weight of aircraft that can operate into or out of the airport or park on available aprons. Sometimes, these limitations may allow higher weight aircraft to operate through the airport but curtail the number of movements over a certain time period applicable to some maximum weight. For example, a concession may be approved for a weight of, say, 80,000 kg, but limited to one such operation per week, or a maximum of six per month.

CREWING

Prior to commencing the operating day, all scheduled flights should ideally be crewed appropriately. To off-set expected crew sickness on the day of operation, appropriate reserve coverage is scheduled at selected airports. Importantly, the expectation by the airline is that all rostered crew members should be adequately rested and fit for duty as well. A further requirement is that they are not under the influence of illicit substances or alcohol and meet all regulatory requirements accordingly. Due to crew training requirements there may be additional crew members on flights. This could be additional Flight Attendants in the cabin who may be under training or may be overseeing trainees or conducting an airline audit on all crew activities during a flight. In the cockpit, a check and training Captain may be overseeing other crew members.

Maximum duty periods including sign-on and sign-off times are prescribed by both the regulator and the airline. In the case of scheduled long-haul flights over, say 12 hours, an augmented (sometimes called 'heavy') crew needs to be rostered for the flight to limit the amount of time the crews spend at the controls. This additional crew complement enables up to 20 hours of duty time (subject to airline work agreements). Future longer haul flights (requiring more than 20 hours crew duty time), will need dispensation. The augmented crew composition then, in addition to the 'normal' crew of Captain and First Officer, may consist of another Captain, or another First or Second Officer, or a Captain *and* First Officer; the latter providing for two complete crews. During these long-haul flights, the crews will take turns to have rest period(s) in the dedicated crew rest area.

MAINTENANCE

Prior to the start of the current day, the IOC expects to operate the schedules with all the planned fleet of aircraft, in a serviceable condition and with no operating limitations. In addition, maintenance equipment and spare parts to support the aircraft in appropriate ports are also expected to be serviceable, and labour sufficient to carry out the planned maintenance activity to be available. That's the theory. However, for many reasons this ideal is not met. In terms of equipment, break-downs do occur, and parts may not be available or in position should they be needed. For example, a GPU needs to be serviceable in the event an aircraft is planned to operate to, or arrives at, a port with an unserviceable APU (auxiliary power unit in the aircraft), in order to be able to start the engines prior to departure.

Aircraft may not be completely serviceable, but are in such a condition that enables them to remain in service. They may, for instance, operate under an MEL which effectively enables the aircraft to fly in specific conditions, but without all components of the aircraft functioning correctly or at all. For example, an aircraft may be authorised to operate with only one of two air conditioning packs serviceable, but may be limited, for example, to 25,000 ft cruise level, which in the case of flying over mountainous terrain, may be an inhibitive factor. Another consideration is that the aircraft will burn additional fuel at this lower level, which may be another factor for the IOC in its preference of where to send the aircraft with this deficiency. Perhaps an anti-ice system is unserviceable, such that the aircraft cannot operate into known icing conditions, or a thrust reverser has been locked out on one engine, which may limit the conditions for landing. In this case, the aircraft may not be able to operate on a wet runway in cross-wind conditions.

In some circumstances, there may be a unique set of procedures that need to be enacted. For example, in what may appear to be a seemingly trivial problem, such as an unserviceable coloured (red/green) navigation light on a wing tip, the aircraft may be able to depart (on an MEL) but in doing so, notification prior to the flight may need to be given to such parties as the airline's Chief Pilot or Duty Pilot, the aircraft manufacturer, control towers at departure and arrival airports, regulators, and en-route ATC. In addition to an MEL, an aircraft might also operate under a CDL. That is, the aircraft can be authorised to depart a port with an external component missing. An example might be a panel or fairing which may be removed but still permit the aircraft to operate, albeit perhaps with speed and/or altitude restrictions. To enable these operations, the airline's maintenance procedures must also ensure licensed Engineers/Technicians 'sign-off' the aircraft in order to be compliant with the manufacturer, regulator(s) and airline's own procedures and processes outlined in their operations manuals. Engineering also have to advise the operating crew and any other personnel deemed to need the information. Operational limitations such as these often result in performance degradation, such that additional fuel may be burnt, schedule duration increased, range reduced, or special clearances needed from ATC.

AIRCRAFT CHARACTERISTICS

Frequent travellers will be mindful of the safety briefing prior to take-off, which includes reference to differences between each aircraft. This is to alert passengers to take heed of the individual peculiarities of each aircraft, referring in particular to the stowage and use of various safety-related equipment. In an operational sense, aircraft units belonging to a specific fleet also differ. An airline that has purchased, say, 30 B737-800 or A320-200 aircraft (i.e., 30 units of the same model), may request the manufacturer to, or may of itself, configure some of these aircraft to meet specific purposes or missions. In addition, airlines that operate a mixture of domestic and international flights may utilise fleet units to serve both networks. For example, an A330 operating New York to Dublin may also serve New York to Denver. The aircraft is likely to be configured (e.g., arrangement of seats, galleys and toilets) and fitted (with in-flight entertainment (IFE), crew rest facilities and work-stations) to facilitate the desired level of service on the airline's international routes.

But the airline may also have the need to use this particular aircraft for some domestic operations, at least for a limited time, perhaps to cover the unavailability of another fleet unit. In this circumstance, changing the characteristics of the internationally configured aircraft would be time or cost prohibitive given the short-term nature of the change and the airline would have to accept the nature of operating a 'non-standard' aircraft. Customers may well notice a significant difference on board too. Another common practice is the chartering of aircraft from another airline or company (such as a leasing company). This may be due to a number of reasons including the airline's own fleet shortages or a number of unserviceable aircraft, a significant capacity requirement beyond the capability of the airline's own resources or may be the result of a major disruption (such as multi-diversions), affecting the airline's own aircraft. In this instance, one solution may be to lease additional capacity to aid the recovery process. Notwithstanding the short-term or even long-term use of externally sourced aircraft, there may be many inconsistencies in configuration, equipment and performance across the airline's own fleet, as shown below.

Instrumentation

The addition or selection of particular flight deck instrumentation may enable specific aircraft to operate within challenging airport environments or in circumstances such as poor weather, or to operate using advanced navigational aids and procedures. RNP-AR (required navigation performance – authorisation required), for example, utilises GPS technology which enables an aircraft to conduct precise approaches into nominated airports, typically those that have problematic surrounding terrain or adverse weather conditions. Other precision approaches such as a CAT III approach also enable an aircraft to operate into and out of specific airports in very low visibility. Aircraft may be fitted with different traffic collision avoidance systems (TCAS). For example, TCAS I provides a proximity warning only, whereas TCAS II analyses and assesses any conflicting flight paths and provides appropriate resolution advisory manoeuvres.

Notably, not all the airline's fleet may be fitted with the same equipment, which means that only selected aircraft may be able to operate on specific routes or into and out of certain airports, thus hampering somewhat the flexibility of solutions available to the IOC. The airline industry continuously strives for two things – safety and cost effectiveness. To achieve these goals, it is continuously improving system support both on and off the aircraft to enable flights to operate anywhere and virtually in any conditions, as safely as possible and with minimal limitation.

Weight limitations

Aircraft are manufactured to, and operate within, a number of weight parameters. Airline Dispatchers and Load Controllers, of course, are aware of these weights and the limitations affecting load capacity and operating performance for all their aircraft.[5] Some aircraft within the fleet may therefore have higher structural weight limits, enabling heavier loads to be uplifted and/or longer distances flown. On the contrary, some aircraft within a fleet may have their weight reduced (e.g., by removing galleys, toilets, seats, or on-board consumables). One consequence of minimising overall weight and thus operating costs, may be beneficial, for example, when the fees attributed to flying through certain airspace or operating through certain airports may relate directly to aircraft weight.

Fuel capacity and consumption

In order to achieve longer flight duration, dedicated aircraft in a fleet may be fitted with additional fuel tanks and/or operate at higher weights (either during the manufacture or retrofitted), enabling them to perform with greater capability on a route than other aircraft of the same fleet. The increase in range achievable may only be incremental but is likely to facilitate perhaps a direct operation or an increased payload and may enable the IOC to favour one aircraft over another in certain circumstances. Of course, this uniqueness can also be counterproductive should the specialised aircraft be unavailable to perform on the chosen route.

The weight of an aircraft also has an effect on the amount of fuel required to be carried, so reducing weight improves fuel burn (usage). Besides the removal of facilities as described above, some aircraft may also have modifications made to their airframes to improve aerodynamics and reduce fuel burn. For example, variously shaped additions or changes to their wingtips (variously called winglets, sharklets, scimitars, etc. depending upon their specific design) may either be fitted by the manufacturer in the case of newly built aircraft or retrofitted to units of an existing fleet. Airlines may be presented with new aircraft deliveries having these adapted designs, in conjunction with their existing fleet. So, preference may be given to utilising such airframes on long-haul routes, in order to save fuel.

Reduced engine thrust

To preserve engine life and help contain maintenance costs, airlines may elect to de-rate engines (by limiting the amount of available thrust) on specific aircraft, with a consequential limit on the performance of the aircraft. Hence, a fleet of one type of aircraft may be fitted with engines of, two power settings; say, 24,000 and 26,000 pounds of thrust. A consequence of this is that aircraft with the lower rated thrust engines may be deemed unsuitable or non-preferred to operate out of certain airports (e.g., those with high elevation, high temperatures, or short runways) or along routes requiring higher levels of performance. This may restrict the working utilisation to some extent. As the cost to modify engines is significant (e.g., US\$1m+), the cost/benefit analysis needs to provide sufficient justification.

Cabin configuration and in-flight entertainment

Certain route economics may call for variations in seat configurations. So, some of the fleet may be configured to offer high-density seating as may be required, for example, in the case of some charter operations, or even the removal of some seats to conduct special missions. The mix of aircraft that comprise just one fleet type can also result in configuration variances. For example, initial deliveries of one type of aircraft may have 180 seats, but further models 186 seats due to a modification, or previous owner's configuration. Other city-pairs with high demand for premium class travel may result in dedicated aircraft with higher numbers of first/business class seats serving primarily on that route. As a result of this, on-board galley equipment and catering requirements may then differ between units. Differences in such equipment, or the inability to offer appropriate catering service to suit the commercial requirement are examples of other limitations placed on IOCs for selecting a particular aircraft for a pattern of flights. Aircraft with differing seat configurations may be preferred for some routes and may be a source of disadvantage should the IOC need to 'downgrade' from a larger to smaller configured aircraft. There could be a passenger offload situation or, in the case of class size changes, a class downgrade for a premium passenger.

In addition, IFE may differ. In some cases, where airlines have brought newly manufactured aircraft into their fleets, or purchased or leased aircraft from other organisations, the IFE may be totally different from the IFE existing in other fleet units. In more recent times, we have observed continuous improvement in technology – emanating from the large, heavy in-flight video systems that took up a considerable amount of area within the cargo hold and provided limited entertainment, reduced now to WIFI systems that are light-weight, take up little space, and provide a diversity of multi-entertainment choices. As a result, overall aircraft weight (hence fuel burn) is reduced, greater belly cargo space enables increased payload, and customer satisfaction is improved.

Crew rest facility

On long-haul flights, crew members (in terms of both Pilot and Flight Attendant groups) must be provided with crew rest facilities. Subject to the length of the flight stage, a number of beds (necessary under regulation for horizontal crew rest) must be provided and located in specially designed, secure areas of the aircraft. Naturally, aircraft configured for such routes will have these facilities included on manufacture, whereas other fleet units of the same type may not. Thus, operations may be limited in terms of which specific aircraft can be utilised for long-haul operations.

Disinsection (or disinfection)

Most countries require disinsection of any aircraft operating internationally. This process is part of the country's biosecurity procedures and typically is carried out at regular intervals. In past times, the passenger cabins of aircraft arriving into some countries may have had to be sprayed by quarantine officers, a process which caused much discomfort for passengers and of course delayed de-boarding. Thankfully, this process rarely occurs and more recently, airlines have had to conform with a certificated process to disinsect their aircraft at regular intervals as part of their ongoing maintenance procedures. Operationally, though, if the airline wishes to swap aircraft between their international and domestic fleets, they have to ensure that a suitably disinfected aircraft is available to operate the international schedule, or should the aircraft not be compliant, a quarantine spraying procedure may still need to be carried out.

Paint schemes

At times, aircraft are painted into specific colour schemes distinct from the standard livery of the airline. This may be for promotions such as special events (Grand Prix, Olympic movement, health or other special causes), the airline's alliance partnership, emphasising indigenous culture, or may reflect the process of updating all company aircraft into a new livery scheme as part of a corporate marketing push. Such promotion may call for specific aircraft to serve a dedicated route structure. In more obscure circumstances, airlines may elect to de-identify their aircraft (by 'whiting' out markings or colours), perhaps for the purpose of a leasing arrangement or for political reasons.

Fleet upgrades

Airlines, from time to time, decide to upgrade their fleet to adapt a changed business model, or in response to competition, or simply to refresh their product offerings as a result of wear and tear. Such an upgrade may range from internal cosmetic changes such as décor, carpets, and seat and head-rest coverings to more significant changes such as a complete seat replacement with new styled seats, or re-designed flat beds that may be slimmer and lighter in weight. The transition of these changes occurs over quite some time (e.g., six weeks per aircraft) as aircraft typically undergo this work as part of their normal maintenance schedule, thus saving the excessive removal of aircraft from the flying patterns.

Ownership and insurance

Airlines that lease foreign aircraft or have within their fleets aircraft that have not been registered in the country may be inhibited from sending that aircraft off-shore, due to the terms of a contract or terms of insurance. This applies not only to airframes but engines as well. With a mixed fleet of owned and leased aircraft, typical of many airlines, restrictions due to these reasons are quite limiting operational factors for IOCs.

Overwater operations

Aircraft operating over expanses of water must, by regulation, carry life rafts of sufficient capacity to house all occupants of the aircraft in the event of an evacuation into water. On some aircraft types, rafts are incorporated in the emergency door/slide system or permanently fitted in part of the aircraft such as the roof cavity or otherwise as per the aircraft's configuration. Once the number of passengers exceeds the fitted life-raft capacity, then additional life rafts need to be loaded. If an aircraft is committed to non-overwater operations, the inclusion of life rafts is not necessary, and to do so would unnecessarily add to the aircraft's operating weight and hence operational cost. However, it will soon be realised that should aircraft changes be conducted, ensuring the appropriate equipment has been fitted to the aircraft then becomes a factor for operational efficiency and maintenance scrutiny.

MISSION SPECIFIC

ETOPS

The requirements and knowledge pertaining to approval of ETOPS flights is a volume (or training course) in itself and well beyond the scope of this text.[6] What is relevant in the context of the IOC here, is the operational availability of an aircraft to perform ETOPS flights and concern for any issue that might prevent or disrupt an otherwise normal operation. One of the primary considerations relating to ETOPS flights,

OPERATIONAL PLANNING AND PREPARATION

of course, is the unlikely incidence of engine shutdown en route and the subsequent need to continue to an alternate airport on a remaining engine(s). IFSD (in-flight shutdown) rate has become extremely low with today's sophisticated engine performance and reliability.

Much of the preparation for ETOPS flights is conducted by Engineering to ensure compliance with the various rules for approval. Of this, the vast majority of maintenance applies to rigorous checking (and servicing where applicable) of items such as, for example, aircraft structure and condition, pertinent systems, alerts and warnings, engine parameters, APU serviceability, technical logs, and MEL and CDL items. More recently manufactured aircraft are certified for increased ETOPS operations (e.g., 240 minutes), which means a lot more redundancy is built into aircraft systems. However, the need for operational serviceability of these items is still critical, and may prevent an aircraft from operating altogether, or limit its operational range or flight path. Due to the nature of ETOPS, airlines may choose to dedicate specific aircraft to these types of operations, which may be satisfactory in terms of scheduling the flights, but limit operational function in the event of unserviceability, especially just prior to departure.

Charter operations

Airlines often have some spare capacity in their fleet to be able to operate charter flights. These are generally for the exclusive use of the charterer (i.e., not available for public sale), and may include charity flights, FIFO (fly in – fly out) flights (see below), perhaps for mining companies. They may also include flights to Antarctica, or even round-the-world sightseeing trips. On occasions, there may be requirements for government or military charters that utilise airline aircraft to fit specific purposes either domestically or internationally. All these operations need unique preparation and the aircraft may need special equipment to fulfil the mission.

Search and rescue (SAR)

At times, airlines may be requested by various authorities to provide an aircraft with crews and observers to conduct a search for, say, a missing person in isolated or inhospitable country, a missing aircraft, or a broken down or distressed vessel at sea. Provision of the resources needed to mount a search operation from the ground may well be contingent on the particular port of origin as well as the schedule enabling an aircraft to be released for the search. Notably, the availability of an appropriate aircraft is important, as it is likely to need sustained endurance to/from a search area, with good capability of remaining on task.

Special operations

On occasions, there may be a need to operate a 'relief' charter. This may be as a result of a devastated region and/or displaced people due to events such as an earthquake, hurricane or tsunami, or for humanitarian reasons as a result of famine, infection or war. Such requests are usually driven by government bodies, whereby assistance from an airline will be sought to provide an aircraft with crews to operate to and from a specified region for a nominated time. For extensive operations, crews may have had to be 'staged' to position them to fly the aircraft for nominated sectors. Ground resources will also have had to be arranged, especially in non-airline ports. In some parts of the world (e.g., some remote parts of outback Australia), significant mining activity calls for numerous charter flights to fly miners in and out of sites (FIFO). These airports are typically barren, with only a sealed runway to permit operations in most weather conditions. However, there is generally no terminal, navigational aids, lighting, fuel, engineering support or ground power. Thus, the IOC, and especially the Engineering function need to ensure that the nominated aircraft for this operation is fit for the mission (e.g., has a serviceable APU to ensure power is available for engine starting), and that no other faults in aircraft systems (e.g., avionics, electrical, hydraulic) are likely to impede the operation. Should the undertaking require a significant time on the ground (e.g., 8 hours), or arrive one day and depart the next, the aircraft needs to be secured at the airport, and the crews accommodated, usually at the mining site.

Politically sensitive operations

In contrast with the above sections, political situations or specific circumstances may emerge that actually prevent an operator from conducting flights to/from or within a particular State at all or preclude an operation with an aircraft identifiable as belonging to a particular airline. Thus, airline markings or colouring may be removed such that the mission becomes a 'white-tail' operation.

CONTINGENCY PLANNING

Final planning just prior to the day of operation will, of course, ensure that the schedule can be performed as expected. The Flight Planning/Navigation functions are a key part of this, resolving any complications or challenges resulting from assessment of the long-range scheduled commitments in particular, and especially those which may encompass operational performance issues (e.g., take-off weight or maximum range problems, and/or potential payload offload situations). Flight plans that are prepared also take into account the primary and secondary diversion ports in the event of some unforeseen circumstance, or indeed, in the case of already known problems such as, for example, adverse weather, volcanic disturbance or regions of political unrest. These en-route potential diversion ports are also checked to ensure they are compliant with company policy and therefore are capable of being used if necessary.

Company fuel policy

There may be requirements to instigate a specific fuel policy affecting some of the operations. Company policy may dictate the uplift of fuel from a specific port such that a return trip can be achieved without refuelling at another port. This may be for price advantage, or to ensure fuel quality. Tankering fuel like this may have financial or quality benefits overall, but also may come at a cost, for example, if a payload restriction is caused by the high onload at the origin. In any case, tankering fuel adds to direct operating costs due to the additional weight of the aircraft on the initial departure.

Fuel policies may also be invoked in the likelihood of fuel restrictions or unavailability. This might mean that additional fuel needs to be carried to avoid refuelling at the first destination with the expectation that fuel will be uplifted at a port beyond (called next port fuel).

FINAL IOC PREPARATIONS – THE HANDOVER

POLICY

As the day of operation gets closer, the schedule should be commercially optimised. That is, the airline has achieved its desired commercial objectives (such as market share, load factor, service levels, etc.) and produced a robust schedule. In addition, all the associated preparatory resources should be fully organised and prepared. Several days from the day of operations (anywhere from 72 hours to perhaps 14 or so days) the IOC takes over the responsibility to fine-tune the plan. In this sense the commercial schedule is being 'operationalised', ensuring that planned maintenance work can be achieved, airport ground-handling capabilities can be met, and that crew pairings and hence rosters satisfy the flying commitments. This window is the time for allocating the aircraft fleet units to the flight patterns that make up the schedule. For international operations in particular, this is most important as aircraft then become committed to patterns that may take them away from the airline's main bases (and therefore, maintenance support) for several days at a time.

The expectation prior to the day of operations is that nothing will be left undone or left to chance. Of course, despite the concerted efforts that lead to this moment, there is always some level of disjoint between the assembly of planned measures and what is actually needed to ensure the highest levels of achievement. Hence, there may be some further manipulation of the schedule to suit contingencies such as operational requirements (e.g., performance issues), environmental issues (e.g., high temperatures, strong winds as discussed above) or perhaps recently issued NOTAMs. Lurking beyond these normal circumstances, of course, are other threats or potentially disruptive situations such as brewing industrial action, political or social unrest, or materialising weather patterns, any of which may serve to affect the schedules about to occur.

THE HANDOVER

With the planning events completed, the final point of note is the handover that takes place once, twice or more each day at numerous locations in the IOC. The outgoing shift may have had a quiet day or night or, alternatively, may have suffered considerable effort with resulting high stress levels due to a series of complex multi-disruptive events. Either way, the handover to the incoming Controller needs to capture the essence of what will drive the next shift. As a result, the briefing usually consists of a recorded (electronic or otherwise) synopsis of events and current or potential status of the airline's operations. Background information would be also available through suitably recorded data, should a historical record be needed.

The handover covers information of primary importance such as following:

a) overall state of the network operation;
b) significant delays, diversions or cancellations;

c) the condition of all the fleet units (i.e., serviceability, defects, limitations, requirements) – this includes aircraft currently under maintenance but perhaps due to return to line flying during the day;

d) non-standard operations – this could include charters (e.g., Antarctic sightseeing), high traffic volume for religious events, or even critical long-haul flights;

e) airport equipment or facilities (e.g., navigational equipment – the loss of an instrument landing system (ILS) may limit an approach procedure); unserviceable GPUs – this is very significant should an aircraft with a U/S APU be scheduled to visit an airport with a U/S GPU, as there may not be any support on the ground for engine start among other needs; unserviceable aerobridges; and fuel availability);

f) any runway, taxiway closure or works, any NOTAMs affecting current of forthcoming operations;

g) weather conditions – both current or expected (e.g., forecast of thunderstorms on the day, or fog overnight);

h) commercial issues (groups travelling, VIPs, CIPs) such as prime flights to be protected, high or low load factors, and any potential offload situations;

i) staffing or other resource issues;

j) other miscellaneous issues.

NOTES

1 Wu, C.-L. 2010. *Airline Operations and Delay Management*, Farnham, Ashgate.

2 *Ibid.*

3 Bazargan, M. 2010. *Airline Operations and Scheduling*, Farnham, Ashgate.

4 IATA Worldwide Slot Guidelines, Part 1: Policy S1.4.1c.

5 For a more complete description of aircraft weight definitions and limitations, see Avery, P. 2018. Aircraft load planning and control, in P.J. Bruce, Y. Gao and J.M.C. King (eds) *Airline Operations: A practical guide*, Abingdon, Routledge, pp. 220–238.

6 For a more complete description of ETOPS, particularly related to Dispatch and flight planning requirements, see Kim, G. 2018. Dispatch and flight following, in P.J. Bruce, Y. Gao and J.M.C. King (eds) *Airline Operations: A practical guide*, Abingdon, Routledge, 239–253.

4 OPERATIONAL PROCESSES

INTRODUCTION

This chapter describes in considerable detail the processes followed on a daily basis within IOCs. With the substantial efforts undertaken to prepare for the day of operation as seen in the last chapter, the actual processes involved in running this day are in a delicate balance. On the one hand, the tools and systems are in place to operate the schedule with the expectation that everything will perform exactly as it is meant to, and that all human, technical and environmental inputs will contribute to, rather than interfere with, the plan. That's the theory. However, anyone who works in the industry or who has flown, will be well aware that so many disruptive factors intervene. This chapter describes the processes involved in regular operations and then illustrates the sheer enormity of what can go wrong, and the cascading effects of these problems on airline assets and resources as well as the flying public.

Operational Authority and Autonomy

Given that an airline has invested in the structure of an IOC and committed to equipping, resourcing and supporting it, a vital element sometimes taken for granted is the nature of autonomy that needs to exist for the IOC to make informed but independent decisions. The IOC is a centre of expertise with substantial power to manage all aspects of the airline's network of flights on a day-to-day basis. The approach of senior management must be to recognise the need for the IOC to have genuine authority to make autonomous decisions without the need for any intercession. In other words, they should be left to get on with their work. However, this is not to suggest that the IOC should operate in a vacuum or not be influenced by company policy or other forms of company direction. Indeed, the IOC needs to have transitioned from being a departmental function to a key instrument entirely charged with airline-focused decisions, and the nature of its integration within the airline structure is of paramount importance.

Systems and Tools

For such a key functional department, the available resources must adequately meet the needs of the task at hand. Hence, the IOC is typically provided with a number of purpose-built systems and tools, often supplied by a variety of software vendors. Although each system is likely to be tailored to suit the requirements of each function, vendors have traditionally specialised in unique products to the extent that integrating these was too cumbersome and costly for airlines. The result was that these independent systems failed to communicate properly with each other. It is only in more recent times that vendors have begun to offer more comprehensive suites of products, but even these are limited in scope or are unable to satisfy the requirements of some functional areas.

COMMUNICATIONS
Between the IOC and aircraft

Efficient and rapid communication is key to information awareness, processing and dissemination, and tools to aid this endeavour are vital to ensure efficiencies are translated appropriately within the operational environment. In the past, communication with aircraft was conducted typically by VHF or HF radio frequencies when available. Sometimes aircraft were out of VHF range and at best HF was limited. Today's fleets are usually fitted with ACARS (aircraft communication addressing and reporting system) equipment, and/or a SATCOM (satellite phone). In non-SATCOM aircraft, crews can use portable devices with WIFI as well. Thus, communication between the IOC and aircraft is achievable continuously and virtually anywhere in the world and so becomes a vital tool in the event the crew need to inform the IOC of any circumstance in relation to the flight, or the IOC needs to make contact with the crew, perhaps to pre-empt some action. This is also a useful tool should a security event emerge during flight.

Within the IOC

Past communication between Controllers and other functional departments such as Crewing and Maintenance was often conducted either by telephone or even relied on physical visitation to those areas with handwritten information or requests – a most inefficient, time-consuming process, and highly subject to error. Modern technologies have greatly enhanced the process and, with sophisticated telecommunications devices, expeditious communication with all the key stakeholders is commonplace. Of course, the physical entity that is the IOC today also means that communication among key stakeholders is not only clear and rapid, but leaves little room for error or misinterpretation, due to the close proximity of the members. The systems shared by the players also enables common understanding of current or emerging activity as will be explained in the following sections.

THE GANTT CHART

The main device used in IOCs has been and still is the Gantt chart, named after its founder, Henry Gantt (1861–1919) who created the tool to assist in planning major infrastructure projects.[1] Numerous vendor suppliers have created and developed aviation-related operations tools, mostly based upon the Gantt chart as its clear displays and copious amount of critical information benefit the viewing, interpretation and manipulation of the flight schedules in a dynamic environment. Information contained within them varies considerably, subject to the airline's specifications and the vendor's capabilities, and there is usually a series of parameters that can be modified by the users such as adapting time scales to suit own preferences, colours and levels of detail, zoom capability, data filtering and

OPERATIONAL PROCESSES

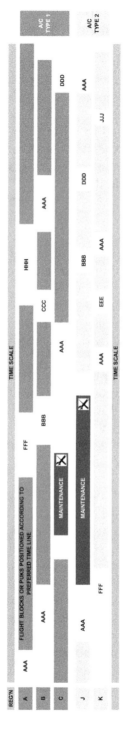

Figure 4.1 Representative Gantt chart

sorting, and several other navigation features. Control and functionality over the Gantt chart normally resides within the IOC, but viewing ability is extended to numerous departments to enable greater awareness of the day of operations. Figure 4.1 presents a representative Gantt chart. In Part II of the text, the Gantt charts will appear larger and in more detail, to support the description of each scenario and enable ready inspection.

Understanding the Gantt chart

The purpose of the chart for operational use is to provide a comprehensive means for displaying the airline's fleet and schedules across a time period. To do this, a matrix structure depicting the airline's flight schedules is built. The schedules are represented by a series of individual blocks (sometimes known as 'PUKs'), which are organised according to departure and arrival times. The fleet of aircraft is displayed on a vertical axis (usually sorted primarily by aircraft type, then further sorted by aircraft registration or tail number). The larger the fleet, the greater the scrolling required to view all of the aircraft. One or more time scales (e.g., UTC/Zulu time or local time as preferred by the user) are sequenced across the horizontal axis. For some airlines, displaying the flights according to the time zone of the IOC's location (e.g., London, Melbourne, Toronto) may be more useful to Controllers within the IOC as they can relate timing of events anywhere in the network to their own location and circumstances. In this case, the flight blocks *display* local departure and arrival times, but may be *positioned* according to the time zone of the IOC's location, as shown in Figure 4.2. Note that for the sake of clarity, the times shown on all Gantt charts throughout the text are rounded to the nearest five minutes. In practice, the scheduled times are subject to (and therefore shown as) specific minutes (e.g., 0738) based on slot or other agreed times.

In contrast, flag or international operators conventionally display flights according to UTC times, as shown in Figure 4.3. An advantage of this standardised approach helps to alleviate any confusion across the network or when communicating with other personnel around the world.

Some systems enable both UTC and local times to be displayed, for ready recognition and mentally adapting communication as appropriate. The ability for individuals to set their own preference emphasises the flexibility needs for designing the software. The series of blocks over a chosen time period (e.g., from a few days to a few weeks) will form each aircraft's line of flight schedules. The schedules will be grouped by aircraft type and then chronologically positioned according to the desired time scale.

OPERATIONAL PROCESSES

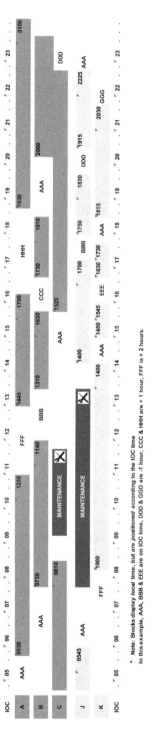

Figure 4.2 Flight blocks positioned according to IOC time zone

OPERATIONAL PROCESSES

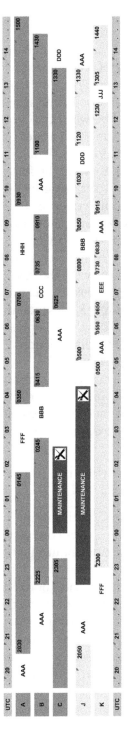

Figure 4.3 Flight blocks positioned according to UTC time zone

The advantage of positioning flights according to departure and arrival time informs Controllers' awareness of the status of flights and assists in their ability to readily identify common operating times, common ground times and other features, any of which may facilitate disruption management. The length of each flight block (horizontal measurement) on the display is governed by the duration of the scheduled flight. For example, a one-hour, short-haul flight between two ports will be represented by a relatively small block. In relation to a predominantly short-haul operator, several such blocks will form each flight pattern usually within a day of operation or extending overnight for 'red-eye' (or 'back of the clock') flights. Examination of the patterns reveals the high number of flights located in a tightly knit sequence, reflecting the levels of complexity common to domestic or short-haul carriers. Figure 4.4 presents an example of a short-haul operation on a Gantt chart.

In contrast, a block representing, say, a 16-hour long-haul flight will span extensively across the display. In the case of a predominantly long-haul operator, several of these types of operations will traverse a number of days on the display. Figure 4.5 presents an example of a long-haul operation on a Gantt chart. Note the compressed time scale.

On most Gantt displays, identifiers denoting the aircraft registrations/tail numbers and blocks representing the line of flying per aircraft are similarly colour coded to facilitate easy identification for the user. So, for example, the registrations/tail numbers and flight blocks of one type of aircraft may be coloured blue, another type coloured green, and another perhaps coloured grey (in this text, shading differentiates the aircraft types).

Information contained within the flight block (sometimes referred to as a PUK)

Subject to the vendor's design and the airline's specifications, the blocks themselves or the surrounding spaces contain sufficient detail to provide Controllers with basic information about a flight. The minimum information will consist of the flight number, scheduled departure time, scheduled arrival time, and passenger load (booked passengers on a flight). The system will also show the ports where the flight is operating to/from. These may appear as additional information on the blocks themselves or more commonly, to reduce clutter, will appear between the blocks. This information may appear to be static on the block, but with the passage of time, changes occur with the progression of both normal and disrupted operations. Once a flight departs, a number of updates take place. If a flight departs on schedule, an actual departure time either

OPERATIONAL PROCESSES

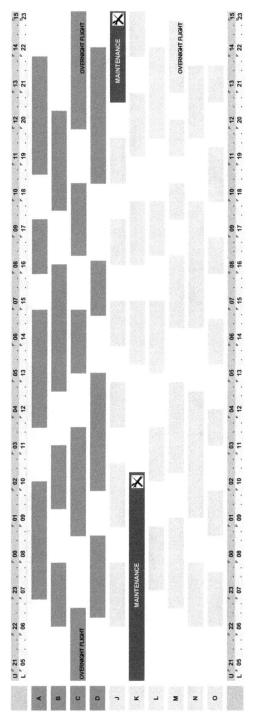

Figure 4.4 Gantt chart representing domestic or short-haul operations

83

OPERATIONAL PROCESSES

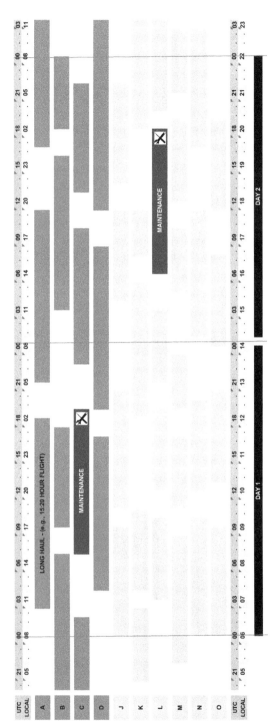

Figure 4.5 Gantt chart representing flag or international operations

84

OPERATIONAL PROCESSES

updates the scheduled time, or appears as additional information on the block, and (subject to the software) the block or part thereof may change to 'green'. If the flight were delayed, say 15 minutes, an additional notation such as a +15 may appear on the block. Delays anticipated, or lack of departure information may be represented by an alert colour such as 'orange', while a 'red' colour may be triggered by a further delay over a certain time. Such display changes are unique to the software and/or airline preference, and accordingly may vary.

Should a flight depart on time, but the estimated arrival time exceed or otherwise differ from the scheduled arrival time, the block may also signify this with a coloured or additional piece of information. Similarly, should an aircraft return to blocks or divert to an airport other than the scheduled destination, the Gantt chart will reflect this activity. Routinely, these changes are *automatically* updated on the displays either by an aircraft's messaging system (such as ACARS), or by a port-generated message source, giving the Controller real-time information and reflecting the most accurate condition of flights under watch. However, Controllers also have the ability to alter details *manually* as the need arises. For example, should a Controller become aware of a delay due to a known maintenance issue, an estimated time of departure can be set for the flight, at which time the flight block concerned, and potentially others, will be updated. Controllers will also alter flight block information should more substantial changes be evident, such as the need to show a flight diversion, cancellation or other event. Figure 4.6 shows an example of the standard information contained on a flight block.

Information contained (explicitly) in the Gantt chart

One of the competing dilemmas in Gantt displays is, on the one hand, the need to provide as much information as possible to facilitate the task, while, on the other hand, the need to simplify the presentation to the user due to the volume of aircraft and flights needing to be displayed on screen together. Despite this, an extensive amount of complementary

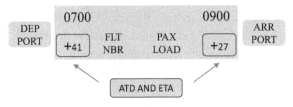

Figure 4.6 Information on a flight block (PUK)

85

information is available. Some of this is explicit (i.e., evident without the need to search). As explained, the flight schedules form the key display but, of course, the space between flight blocks is important as this indicates the times where an aircraft is on the ground. Ground time may range anywhere from the shortest scheduled turnaround time provided by the Scheduling function for the specific aircraft in a specific port (perhaps even down to 15 minutes in some cases), to far longer, where an aircraft may be uncommitted for several hours or more. The significance of these ground times or gaps in the utilisation, seen as blank or white spaces on the Gantt chart, are readily sought after by Controllers, as uncommitted aircraft can provide a valuable source of capability should disruptions occur. The gaps may provide suitable buffers where late-running schedules can be recovered due to the longer ground time, or they may expose opportunities to swap aircraft patterns as one method for containing delays or solving some other problem. Should a minimum turnaround time be compromised (e.g., as a result of a delayed arrival), an alert may be triggered indicating some intervention is necessary.

Another important feature contained in the display is the inclusion of maintenance information. This information can be represented in a number of ways. Should a requirement be for a significant duration, such as maintenance work (e.g., an aircraft wash), a maintenance service (e.g., Check A), or a component change (e.g., an engine, windscreen, carpet), the representation on the Gantt chart is often a long, coloured placard stretching across the day or night, often in a distinguishing 'red' or 'purple' colour, to avoid similarity with flight blocks, as shown in Figure 4.7.

Maintenance work of a shorter duration may be represented by a smaller placard, again coloured distinctively, and often evidenced by a small icon. Alerts and violation warnings also appear as Maintenance icons, denoting perhaps checks to be performed or time-critical inspections to be carried out, as seen in Figure 4.8.

Information contained (implicitly) in the Gantt chart

Besides the static appearance of the Gantt chart at first glance, using methods such as hovering over parts of the display, or 'mouse-clicking' at selected hotspots, produces additional information about a flight or series of flights. High on the list of information needed in a disruptive situation are details about passenger connections (tranships), both inbound connecting *to* a nominated flight, or outbound connecting *from* a flight. Figure 4.9 presents an example of an expanded set of passenger connections on the Gantt chart. Notably, connections to and from a specific flight can be displayed.

OPERATIONAL PROCESSES

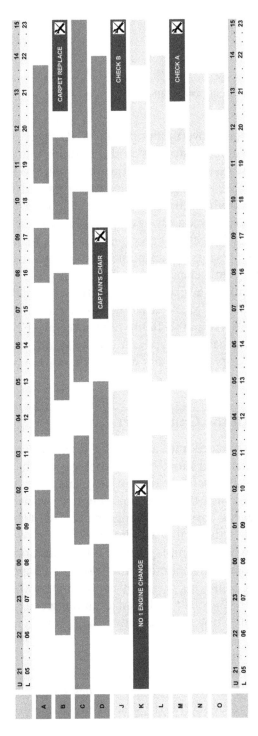

Figure 4.7 Representation of extended maintenance work

OPERATIONAL PROCESSES

Figure 4.8 Representation of maintenance icon

In addition, customer-recovery options can be displayed showing several flights on which disrupted customers can be accommodated.

In a similar vein, crew names, qualifications, connections, duty commitments perhaps with sign-on/sign-off times and maximum duty hours included (for both Technical Crew and Flight Attendants) can be displayed. Further exploration can reveal information such as names and numbers of specific connecting crew members and associated information. Figure 4.10 presents an example of an expanded set of crew connections on the Gantt chart.

Other information available to Controllers relates to aircraft configurations, passenger break-down by travel class (i.e., F, J, Y), fuel uplift and burn, and estimated flight time interval (FTI). If information is needed other than what appears on the Gantt chart, Operations Controllers can access other data sources or communicate with the appropriate personnel.

Design features of the Gantt chart

Most Gantt displays incorporate a zooming function, enabling users to scrutinise a particular operation, or part thereof within a specific timeframe, which could be useful in disruption management. Alternatively, users may 'zoom out' if seeking a more complete overview of the flight commitments of several days. Depending on the size of the fleet, another important function is the ability to filter the display to capture event-specific information. For example, should a fog situation be highly disruptive in a particular port, filtering the display to capture operations through that port only for a specified time period would enable Controllers to ensure they had gathered a unique set of critical information and, importantly, not excluded anything. However, as mentioned in an earlier chapter, they need to have full oversight of the network so as not to unintentionally preclude the identification of related information. Given the extent of some fleets, extensive vertical scrolling may be needed to enable all the airline's schedules to be observed readily. Similarly, the storage of several days' schedules enables Controllers to

OPERATIONAL PROCESSES

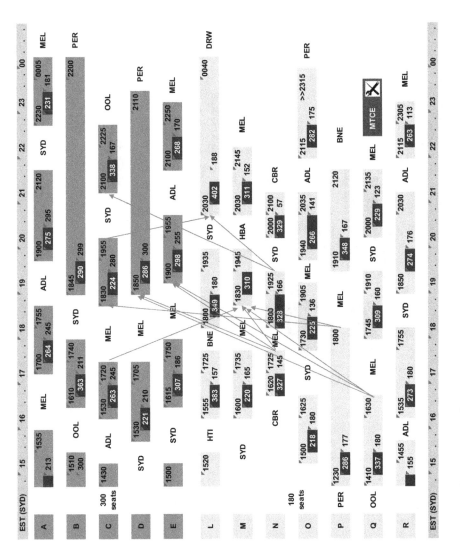

Figure 4.9 Depiction of customer connections

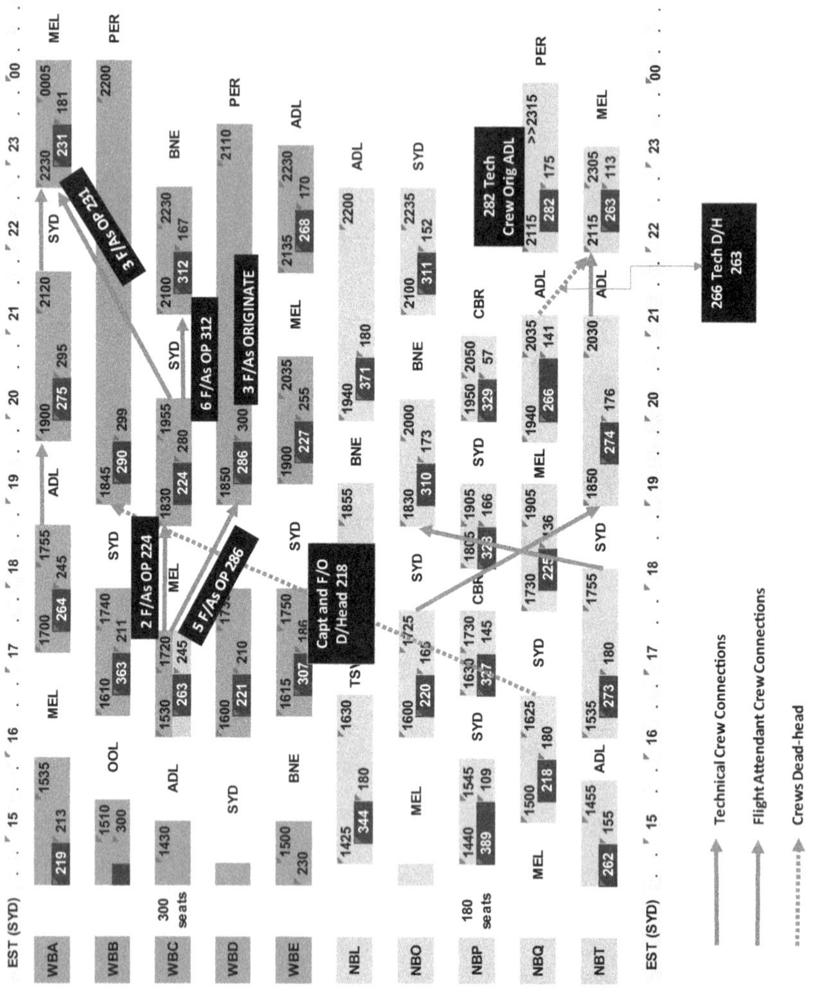

OPERATIONAL PROCESSES

Figure 4.10 Depiction of crew connections

OPERATIONAL PROCESSES

scroll ahead (horizontally) to observe long-term pattern commitments, or perhaps to explore opportunities to address particular problems that can't be resolved in the short term.

Dynamic change in the Gantt chart

Recognition of time progression is indicated on the Gantt chart by a moving timeline. This is a vertical line coupled to the current time, from which Controllers can quickly ascertain the current status of the airline's network of flights, as shown in Figure 4.11.

Flight status progression is indicated by changes to times, changes in colour and various alert functions that appear on or near the flight blocks. This advice is most likely informed through an aircraft's ACARS system or other means as explained earlier. In addition, some system notifications may be sent directly to Controllers (e.g., a system-generated note/email). As a flight departs, some indication of the actual departure time will be presented by a change on the flight block, with the estimated

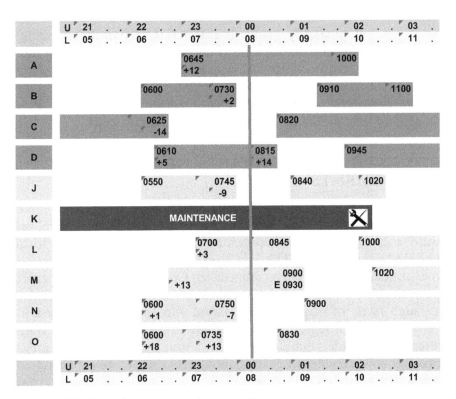

Figure 4.11 Gantt chart incorporating a timeline

time of arrival (ETA) then updated at the end of the block. Should changes to the ETA be incurred during flight (e.g., caused by ATC, headwinds, tailwinds), other sources such as ATC or airline staff at ports can advise the IOC to ensure updates are made to the Gantt chart.

Manipulating the Gantt chart

Of course, the power behind the Gantt chart is its ability to display the current status of the aircraft flight patterns such that current and future operations are clearly identifiable. Therefore, changes that are necessary due to some form of disruption or request, however minor, must be readily updatable. For example, a series of diversions due to a weather situation needs to be reflected promptly on the Gantt chart to enable observers to gain a fresh insight into the changed circumstances and take into account any impact on their own workplace.

Another important feature is the ability for the IOC to conduct 'what-if' scenarios for the purpose of testing decision strategies for workability, and/or proposing solutions to other areas such as the Crewing functions to assist them in envisaging the implications of any change. Controllers can physically manipulate the Gantt chart by selecting, dragging and dropping flight blocks using a combination of mouse and keyboard selections. Changing the display in this way not only updates the aircraft patterns, but also serves to alert the user of any planned commitments for aircraft such as maintenance work should, for example, a long ground time period or an end of day base be disrupted.

BEYOND THE GANTT CHART – NEW DEVELOPMENTS

While the Gantt chart has provided a useful tool for decades, rapid improvements in digitisation and data analytics are underpinning moves toward a different and perhaps more valuable platform to perform operations management.[2] This is a most welcome development and is actively under consideration at airline level. Criticisms of the Gantt chart have included a number of inefficiencies, lack of properly integrative data, high levels of manual interpretation and application, and a reliance on obsolete or segregated technologies. From the detailed sections written above, readers should be well aware of the importance, significance and considerable detail contained within the more sophisticated examples of Gantt charts in use in IOCs, at least in historical terms. Whichever directions developing technologies take future platforms and tools for application within the IOC, key aims are still to inform human decision makers with the optimal information at crucial times to enable the most appropriate decisions. Whether airlines persist with the Gantt chart as the primary tool for economic reasons, system integration or simply human preference, or transpose to alternative platforms remains to be seen, but the expertise that resides in the IOC is still fundamental in the decision-making process.

SOFTWARE RELATING TO OTHER FUNCTIONAL AREAS WITHIN THE IOC

As much as the Gantt chart provides the predominant tool for managing the schedules on an operating day, a suite of other products serves to facilitate other functions within the IOC. This software is specialised, applying to the key areas of Crewing, Maintenance, and perhaps Flow Control. In some airlines, the Operations Controllers may have sets of unique information to complement the displays on the Gantt chart, thus providing all the information (albeit separate) in one convenient location. Of course, specific and detailed information is forthcoming from other function teams, but with one quick glance, a summary position is achievable although with varying degrees of integration.

COMPLEMENTARY TOOLS

In addition to the tools mentioned above, the IOC may make use of several other tools available for monitoring aircraft movements or status, from the simplest such as a display of a series of clocks in the IOC signifying current times at operating ports all over the network, or TV screens monitoring current affairs or world events raising awareness, for example, of political hotspots or other events with potential to disrupt operations. Besides direct radio or satellite-phone communications with aircraft, IOCs may also be able to monitor ATC frequencies to provide them with accurate information with respect to aircraft positions, especially those holding inbound or even on the ground, and calculating landing times.

Many ports incorporate cameras on the apron, or other movement areas to facilitate shared vision of aircraft arrival, handling and departure activity. In some cases, airports mount cameras along runways, or at runway thresholds. This provides a number of stakeholders including airline IOCs with an ability to discern aircraft ground traffic issues such as congestion or blocked taxiways. Another advantage may be to provide an enhanced meteorological observation, particularly when minimal weather conditions such as fogs are likely to affect take-offs and/or landings. Frontline staff now use hand-held digital devices to conduct much of their work, especially when 'out of office' on the ramp such that instant two-way communication and data transfer becomes available. Other commercially available tools exist for monitoring operating flights around the world. Again, IOCs in real-time are able to observe disruptions with the potential to impact upon their operations, such as aircraft in extensive holding patterns, or in the process of being re-routed, or diverting. This information can generally be filtered to limit the data to specific operators and fleet types.

Network status – OTP

Several airlines have a number of current-state performance displays located within the IOC. These typically contain summary information about the status of the operating day across their network or, if needed, at key airports – especially the airline's critical hubs. Using a 'dashboard' symbolism incorporating a series of colour coded 'tachometer-like' indicators (e.g., with green for on-time, orange for probable delays, and so forth, with accompanying percentage figures), performance of movements can be readily identified. Thus, a glance at the dashboard can very quickly render considerable information about an airline's on-time performance, and in particular specific arrival and departure perform-ance at a port or ports, any ground-holding times, dispatch reliability, and current or historic diversions and cancellations. In addition, con-temporary systems can often break the data further into more mean-ingful information for IOC management, by separating the metrics into, for example, international, domestic or subsidiary operations.

Weather status – current or developing

Several weather events have the potential to affect operations, including current or developing weather systems (such as typhoons/hurricanes/cyclones, tornados, volcanic ash clouds, frontal and tropical thun-derstorm activity, and areas of turbulence and icing conditions). To monitor such events, weather displays covering parts of a country, focused in a particular region, or on affected airports can provide signi-ficant information. For example, a weather watch may be in progress, monitoring the development and track of an approaching hurricane; hence the importance of housing a qualified Meteorologist within the IOC (see Chapter 2). As part of a daily (or more frequent) briefing process, the IOC will consider this information several days ahead of likely disruptions as a means of assessing potential impact on the schedules. In the case of a significant event such as flooding, wild (or bush) fires, an approaching major winter storm, volcanic disturbance or other, action can then be taken to remove flights, and perhaps position aircraft, crews and ground staff likely to be affected. In severe cases, the assessment might also provide for relocating the IOC function itself together with its staff, to a back-up site. Hence, system redundancy is an important design aspect of IOC management.

Maintenance status

A summary of current maintenance unserviceabilities or restrictions placed on aircraft may be displayed on a maintenance status board. For example, there might be a listing of the maintenance equipment available and serviceable at airports. Should the sole GPU not be serviceable at a particular port, only aircraft with serviceable APUs should operate to that port. Maintenance items pertaining to aircraft also will be indicated, especially if they affect the planned operation of specific aircraft during the day or forthcoming period. There may be a request or requirement for a specific aircraft registration to operate into an overnight base for some repair or servicing work. An aircraft unserviceability covered by an MEL, or a configuration deviation (covered by a CDL) may restrict the performance of the aircraft, perhaps limiting its speed or cruising altitude or limiting the routes and/or airports to which it may operate. Some of these items will be denoted on the Gantt chart but the advantage of the status board is its capability as a quick reference resource.

REGULAR OPERATIONS

Every day in every airline is different. Even if all is seemingly quiet with no or minimal disruption, the schedules, weather, maintenance requirements, air traffic flows, port resources, crews, aircraft, payloads, operating restrictions, and of course customers are different each operating day. So, no two days will ever present in the same way. In addition, people's psychological states, moods and behaviours all change from day to day, so the way they prepare, approach and carry out work, of course, varies. Even if the network is quiet (i.e., flights are operating on or very close to schedule), the day-to-day operation still demands attention. In airlines, the incidence of regular operations usually means handling the schedules as presented

OPERATIONAL PROCESSES

but always with the mindset that things will go wrong. That is, the expectation on shift is that irregular operations are really the norm. However, on the assumption of no current disruption evident, the following sections reveal the levels of activity that should be taking place.

PROACTIVE APPROACH

Following the handover from the previous shift, which may have concluded at any time around the clock, a whole new set of people will start to brief themselves on the status of the operation; checking company policies, current status boards indicating any issues concerning maintenance or weather conditions, or route or airport restrictions, as well as gathering any other information as necessary from a number of appropriate sources. Status indicators may also reflect current airline performance in terms of delays, cancellations, congestion, load factors or similar items. At a quick glance, Controllers can get a feeling for the overall condition of the airline. If the handover consists of a screen (or paper record) of historical logs and alerts for the upcoming operations, these will be assessed with some priority. As the current primary tool, the status of the Gantt chart and other key resources will be a key focus at this stage, as Controllers seek to build initial awareness of the current schedule. If the operation is sound, there should be nothing out of the ordinary on the utilisation. Typically, previously operated flights may present on the Gantt chart as dimmed or greyed out, and unless the handover process draws attention to any significant issue, are not likely to be of any regard in the briefing process.

In the case of a domestic, short-haul or predominantly day operation airline, the handover in preparation for the morning shift (which could begin anywhere, for example, from 0500 to 0700), requires a level of scrutiny and emphasis on specific aspects that may differ somewhat. For example, with much of the network operation commencing at about 0600–0700 (as this is the time range that demand – especially business travel, typically warrants and curfews allow) there is a substantial focus on ensuring this 'first wave' gets under way. Thus, the Controllers and the functional specialists in the IOC will all be particularly interested in factors such as weather that might affect departures, aircraft serviceability, crew 'sign-on times', airport terminal activity, ATC issues and so forth. In general, though, the familiarisation stage for the new shift calls for a proactive approach which means a fairly rigorous examination of the Gantt chart, taking into account several considerations. The points below are all important, but their order of inspection or priority really depends on the Controller.

OPERATIONAL PROCESSES

a) Scanning the utilisation on the Gantt chart will provide a general overview. The Controller assesses each line of aircraft pattern of flying, looking for potential delays or any unusual precursors that might lead to problems. Besides focusing on the flight blocks themselves, what should also attract attention are the size of the gaps between flights. These are turnaround (or turn) times. If they are very short; that is, an aircraft is only on the ground between flights for a minimum time, this would indicate to Controllers that a delay to the first service is likely to result in a consequential delay to the subsequent one, unless some change can be invoked. On the other hand, if they are long, this presents opportunities to recover late-running flights by absorbing some of the excess ground time or presents opportunities to change aircraft patterns for any number of reasons.

b) Patterns that are running delayed may also be threatening to break curfews at the end of the day in specific curfew ports (note: most curfews commence at 2300 and end at 0600 – see Chapter 3 for further description). In some regions, rather than curfew restrictions, control towers may close. The effect is the same, though – operations generally cease at closure time. Due attention will be given to these patterns and the flights therein will be monitored across the day, with a view to preventing any curfew/tower breach. On some patterns, changing aircraft is impossible without causing delays, as multiple aircraft patterns may never coincide during the day, but in such cases this or more significant action may be required, such as accepting a sizeable delay or, in extreme cases, cancelling a service.

c) The Controller will also need to be aware of any planned maintenance work to be carried out on aircraft. For international (flag) carriers, as the schedule operates day and night, and turnaround times can sometimes be extensive (e.g., 15 hours), some maintenance work will be carried out during the daytime. In contrast, schedules of domestic carriers tend to be conducted within a day, with far less call in general for overnight flights. That, and the fact that many ports may be curfew restricted, result in a large proportion of maintenance work (e.g., service checks, engine and other component changes) being carried out at night. This work will display as icons or some other symbology on the Gantt chart to alert Controllers should disruptions affect the specific aircraft. Controllers also need to consider the arrival times of the last flights into those ports where the maintenance work is to be performed, so as to ensure sufficient overnight time and without any consequence to departures the next day. Naturally, the Maintenance Watch personnel will also be aware of planned work and will therefore be monitoring flights during their shift.

OPERATIONAL PROCESSES

d) Flights that are lightly loaded (i.e., small number of booked customers) may be identified as being potential candidates for delays or cancellations in the event of any future disruption. This is because the customer load will usually be able to be accommodated on other flights, and there is a greater need for the aircraft on an alternative service.

e) In contrast, flights that are heavily loaded may be deemed as being given priority over other flights as accommodating those customers on alternative services is more difficult. Of course, selecting flights to be delayed or cancelled doesn't just rely on the passenger loadings. There may be several other considerations such as the next commitment for the aircraft, crew patterns, or maintenance issues, for example.

f) Special operations (see Chapter 3) may include charters (e.g., Antarctica), searches, ferry flights (positioning flights with no passengers), delivery flights (for new aircraft) and so forth. Controllers will be aware of the numerous organisational factors and personnel involved in each of these and the need to give them due attention. Although commonplace, ultra-long-range flights draw the attention of Controllers and Dispatchers alike due to the critical nature of their operation. Monitoring of these operations is continuous and exacting as disruption recovery brings about significant challenges. Awareness of operations into politically sensitive or dangerous 'hotspots' of the world also calls for careful consideration. Most often the briefing given to Controllers includes updates from the appropriate authority, as well as current airline management policy. Nevertheless, operations into or across these regions need due deliberation.

g) The Commercial or CJM areas may be sensitive to disrupting specific routes or flights due to the frequency or effects of previous disruptions, so some protection may be afforded those flights by Controllers in the event of disruption. Part of this team's work is to identify and monitor the VIP/CIP lists, advising Controllers where appropriate. Although carriage of such important passengers may not necessarily pre-determine a particular decision, it may certainly have some influence.

h) The introductory section above raised the question of weather conditions affecting the first wave of departures. Part of the briefing includes a thorough assessment of any weather situations likely to affect the operations over the forthcoming period. Clearly, the forecast of a blizzard, or typhoon (or equivalent name), for example, will be well known prior to the day of operation, as described earlier. But of more regular concern for day-to-day operations are conditions such as fog, thunderstorm activity, strong winds and high temperatures.

Subject to the seasons, mornings and afternoons may also produce significantly different weather phenomena. A potential problem area might include a weather front with thunderstorms and heavy rain expected to pass through a major port, which would instigate a pre-emptive assessment of likely impact. Another may be a customer off-load situation several hours away in relation to a scheduled long-haul flight operating from a high elevation or high-temperature airport. This is likely to initiate discussion between the Controller and Flight Planning/Load Control or Dispatch areas, for example.

As they explore the vagaries of the information at hand, Controllers actively use this opportunity to build pictures in their minds, getting a 'feel' for the airline, judging if any threats appear to exist, or weaknesses that may be exploited, and playing out 'what-if' scenarios, should disruptions occur. The intuitive, experienced Controller makes the most of this effort, and the result pays dividends when disruptions eventually occur, as they are already 'armed'. This is valuable time. The more sustained the proactive work during such unusual periods of quiet, the better prepared all Controllers will be in the event of disruption. Once sound awareness of the operational status is gained, Controllers can then become a little more relaxed and confident of the initial control gained, at least until an event occurs. Of course, beginning a shift in the midst of turmoil, can be quite different and is more the focus of the second part of the book.

Downtime

There may also be times during a shift when ongoing or emerging disruptions are either negligible or fairly innocuous, at which point the task then becomes largely a monitoring (and wait and see) approach. The level of activity across the IOC falls and inter-communications quieten as well. This downtime enables routine tasks to be fulfilled amid a quieter environment devoid of the intensity that often prevails during disruptions. These are valuable opportunities and may indeed serve as short recovery periods for fatigued or drained staff. Accordingly, it is important that Controllers are not side-tracked or diverted into involvement in other undertakings. Circumstances such as these are rather rare, and the respite needs to be protected somewhat. A further consideration is that even if the schedule is operating on or close to on-time, this doesn't mean that personnel are idle in the IOC. Even if there are no disruptions current, a lot of other work is still being performed. For example, the Crewing

OPERATIONAL PROCESSES

function may be busy covering crew sickness or other shortfalls, and Maintenance may be re-organising work packages or changing maintenance planning commitments due to other influences.

IRREGULAR OPERATIONS (IROPS)

Despite the rigorous planning that precedes a day of operation, there are innumerable factors that challenge the integrity of the schedule. Some disruptions are very minor in themselves, and can be absorbed and often isolated quite readily, with little or no ongoing effect to the greater schedule. More often than not, though, disruptions are not as neat and simple. Many times, they can be frustrating for Controllers as seemingly trivial issues (e.g., lost paperwork, flat aircraft torch battery, lack of crew meals) cause delays every day to every airline. But typically, problems tend to become quite complex, and frequently have far-reaching effects, both with regard to the day of operation, and often with roll-on effects into the next and subsequent days. For example, a significant problem with an international fleet operating long-haul may take four to five days for the schedules to be fully recovered and aircraft returned to their planned patterns. There may be immediate indications such as delays, diversions, threatened curfews, stranded passengers, aircraft out of position, crews both out of position and out of duty hours, and there may be an emerging series of consequences, largely unforeseen (as illustrated in this real case scenario).

> What may begin seemingly as a simple issue (e.g., high-speed tape required for a cockpit window seal – a fairly straightforward maintenance issue), can translate into several consequential actions. In this example, the procedure required a sign-off from the aircraft manufacturer to approve the aircraft to operate. Due to the tight aircraft patterns (i.e., numerous flights with short ground or turn times) and to minimise a probable delay while this approval was being organised, a subsequent aircraft change was made to protect the schedule (using the same aircraft type), but resulting in a heavily fuelled aircraft (initially intended to operate a long-haul flight) being committed onto a short-haul sector. The Operating Captain of this short-haul sector advised that this aircraft was now overweight for landing due to the swap, necessitating either a defuel (involves recalling the fueller – if and when available, and then a lengthy process to defuel) or an

offload of passengers and baggage (involves selecting passengers to offload based on class of travel, loyalty level, or some other method). Either way, a further delay resulted.

Not only may isolated disruptions propagate across a number of flights, but ironically several disruptions often tend to occur simultaneously, resulting in a vastly more significant network-wide effect. The IOC then becomes a hive of activity as the expertise is called upon to manage the situation. The approach by the IOC for managing the disruption is subject to the timing of problems, and likelihood of their emergence as threats to the schedule. These factors can be categorised according to risk; is there a likelihood of occurrence? If there is, what is expected to occur and when? What is happening right now? What has already happened that needs IOC attention? What resources are needed both now, and in the future? These and other issues are explored further below.

Operational Actions and Strategies

With the knowledge that disruptions are inevitable, there are only so many tactics an IOC can employ in response.[3] As has been emphasised earlier, the contemporary focus is well and truly upon customer journey management – reducing or eliminating threats that interrupt customers' travels or recovering operations in the light of problems that have occurred. So, any responses take this into account, even if they may appear to be affecting some parts of the schedule quite harshly. One prime task of the IOC is to balance the needs of the network and doing this may at times result in significant disruption to some specific flights or regions. Indeed, a primary value of the IOC is this oversight and appreciation of control over the entire system.

In terms of exacting the cost of disruptions, most of these can be quantified – accommodation, transport, phone charges, meal vouchers, customer re-bookings and so forth are easily tracked. But airlines have always struggled with accounting for 'customer cost'. Here, the question of customer loyalty is most difficult to judge. As indicated in the first chapter, the historical approach may well have been to recover the aircraft patterns, and then resolve the passenger upheaval and fallout as a consequence. Now, with such an unrelenting focus on customer satisfaction and appeasement in times of disruption the cost of, say, ferrying an aircraft from A to B in order to retrieve a scheduled operation may be of far less significance than the more crucial cost of losing customer loyalty because a particular recovery plan that may have suited the airline, was unacceptable to the customers.

The most common action, well known to passengers, is a flight *delay*. Flights delayed by less than 15 minutes are considered on schedule under international standards, and delays are reported to a number of organisations and/or government. Thus, airline performance is partly measured (and reported) according to its on-time performance (OTP), both in terms of departure and arrival performance. While the IOC will seek on-time departures, delays are inevitable, and often the result of numerous contributing factors. What will be addressed though, is the opportunity to isolate delays to the minimum number of flights to stop further spread across the network. Flights that are significantly delayed, or threaten to propagate widely, may require more firm action such as one or more *cancellations*. The disruption to passengers may be more harmful with a cancellation, subject to alternative uplifts being available, but may overall be the most efficient method to simplify or minimise impact. Cancelling one service also implies a balancing action of some form to normalise the schedules. This could amount to creating an additional flight in the same direction, or cancelling a flight in the opposite direction, or some other action or set of actions.

Some disruptions certainly call for *additional* flights, either as revenue (enabling the carriage of passenger/freight, and therefore requiring a full cabin crew) or *ferry* (non-revenue) flights which are conducted with pilot-only crews. Some IOCs seek to minimise ferry flying as this is not only expensive but produces no income for the airline. However, offsetting this is the requirement to position aircraft appropriately to operate other revenue flights that may not otherwise have been able to operate. Finally, *diversions* occur for many reasons. A 'simple' diversion (e.g., for fuel due to headwinds – sometimes known as a technical stop) is relatively innocuous and, other than being inconvenient, is usually a matter of re-dispatching the flight. It must be remembered that with the more recent increase in ultra-long-haul flying, a diversion en route for fuel or other reasons is likely to render the crew out of hours (such that the total flight time would then exceed their ToD (tour of duty) limitation). This would necessitate either crew rest and a subsequent lengthy delay, or the positioning of a replacement crew (however possible) to the diversion port, to bring the aircraft onward. On the other hand, multiple diversions that occur due to a major weather situation, for example, call for more strategic thinking to relocate the aircraft (and crews, passengers, etc.) and minimise overall disruptive effects. Avenues for manipulating late-running or otherwise disruptive schedules may include identifying opportunities to swap aircraft, which could involve similar aircraft types (i.e., two or more aircraft registrations/ tails belonging to the same fleet) or substituting between types (i.e., wide-body for narrow-body or vice versa, or further, a change of aircraft according to their manufacture).

IMPACTING FACTORS

Whatever the strategy or action adopted, the IOC is well aware of the costs involved: cancellations may save delays as well as fuel and perhaps crew costs but may cost loyalty should passengers defect. Ferry flights may be expensive to operate but may be the only means of relocating an aircraft in position to operate revenue flying. The following categorisation of disruptions illustrates the common problems or irregular operations that occur and the IOC responses using such operational strategies.

POTENTIAL DISRUPTIONS

In the vast majority of cases, problems can be identified and assessed as to their likely impact on the network. A large and highly proactive role of the IOC is scanning ahead to explore potential areas of risk for the airline. Potential disruptions may occur for any number of reasons, such as, for example, threatened industrial action in three days' time (e.g., a looming Air Traffic Controller strike within one of the countries to which the airline operates or overflies), an approaching major weather pattern such as a typhoon (termed cyclone or hurricane subject to the region of the world) that is building 200 kilometres off a coast, an extensive snowstorm moving toward an airline hub, an active volcanic eruption, or perhaps a manufacturer's or regulator's early warning to impose some maintenance AD (Airworthiness Directive) requiring aircraft rectification by a certain date. Each of these events calls for due attention in terms of the likelihood of eventuality and contingent effect on operations. Thus, the IOC will summon a number of resources and conduct a risk analysis, with the intent to mitigate the effect of, or better still if possible, circumvent the occurrence altogether.

OPERATIONAL PROCESSES

IOC Response Patterns (General)

In the descriptions below of potential and imminent disruptions, the IOC responses allude solely to the category of disruption. This is to avoid overly repetitive material. However, it needs to be clearly signified first that *any* disruption that occurs leads (or at least *should* lead) Controllers to consider a fundamental set of questions. These are as follows:

a) If a flight is delayed, what is the effect on the *customer*? (This is now the first and foremost thought – the rest may be contingent upon the answer to this question). This includes the question of customer *tranships* (connecting customers to other flights). If connections appear to be threatened by the delay, what is the next availability for customer recovery – either with this or an alternative airline?
b) What *consequences* for other flights will be caused by this delay and can they be contained or limited in some way?
c) What is the *aircraft*'s next commitment? Can this be changed if necessary?
d) What are the *Technical crews*' next commitments and their ToD limitations? Are there alternative crews?
e) What are the *Flight Attendant crews*' next commitments and their ToD limitations? Are there alternative crews?
f) Is any *curfew* threatened? If so, what are some options to avoid this risk?
g) What planned *maintenance* tasks may be affected? Can these be retrieved?

There are many more areas for consideration, but these primary ones serve to underpin the basic question set applicable for any disruption. Given these responses, the additional actions pertaining to the management of specific events are more localised. In some cases, responses may be common, but in others, they can be unique.

Weather

Weather situations are probably the most challenging for the IOC. Several types of weather conditions affect operations, including fog, cloud, winds, temperatures, thunderstorms, tornados, en-route icing conditions, typhoons/cyclones/hurricanes, ice and snow. Weather

OPERATIONAL PROCESSES

situations occur somewhere within an airline's network on a daily basis. An IOC is either planning for, or is already operating in, such an environment. Weather conditions may fluctuate slightly or change significantly; either having an impact on operations. For example, should an aircraft be ready to depart, or worse, have already departed, and the weather, say, at the destination, deteriorates to near or below minimal landing conditions, subject to the amount of fuel uplifted the aircraft may have to return to the gate, or if already airborne, consider returning to the departure port, or divert to an en-route port. Weather can also have a compounding impact. For example, the weather at a port may be at or above minimum conditions at the time a number of aircraft arrive on station (in the area), but a combination of required instrument approaches and the subsequent build-up of air traffic due to ATC holding, means that they may need to divert without even attempting an approach. The aircraft may well have uplifted sufficient fuel to allow for the weather situation, but not to cater for extensive ATC holding imposed as well. Any one of these options is disruptive, which is a key reason that Meteorologists, Dispatchers and Controllers in the IOC, as well as the operating crew and airport staff, need to be aware of these sorts of conditions and hopefully any worsening trends. Despite the considerable planning to avoid situations like this, occasionally airlines can get caught (as this illustration depicts).

> An aircraft departed a port compliant (i.e., carrying sufficient fuel with reserves but not carrying alternate fuel) in accordance with current and forecast weather at the destination. While en route though, the weather (fog) at the destination worsened considerably, and it was determined the aircraft did not have sufficient fuel to hold at the destination, return to the departure port, or reach any other major ports. Accordingly, the aircraft diverted to a smaller regional airport within range. However, the weather at that alternate airport had also deteriorated (fog), and the airport did not have appropriate navigational equipment for the aircraft to perform the necessary precision instrument (e.g., ILS) approach. After one missed approach, the aircraft declared an emergency and eventually landed safely.

The situation may be more critical for flag or international operators with long-haul flights, where poor weather conditions at the destination raise the likelihood of diversions. Some operators will carry whatever fuel is necessary to cover the trip and alternate requirements, at the expense

105

of payload, whereas others work to a decision-divert policy. In this case, rather than return to their origin, or divert early in the flight, they are likely to continue as far as operationally practicable. The weather can be quite changeable (worsening or improving), and in some cases, the flight may not even have to divert if conditions improve sufficiently. But, if they do divert en route, they will usually choose from a number of possible listed (i.e., company stipulated) diversion ports nominated during the flight-planning stage, and will elect to use one of these, all things being equal. Sometimes, though, in an extreme situation, it may be necessary to divert to a non-listed and even a non-airline serviced port. The latter brings about a whole raft of new problems such as ground-handling concerns, passenger accommodation, and recovery of the aircraft and crew to resume the flight as soon as possible. In the case of diverting into an airport in a country not normally serviced, or with particular security or other concerns, another issue is the approval processes that need to be exercised in order to depart that airport and traverse the foreign airspace; sometimes requiring government intervention.

COMMON WEATHER FACTORS

The following headings relate to the most common weather conditions affecting airline operations. Each category considers the type of weather condition, effect on operations and the IOC responses for likely actions.

FOG

Fog is one of the most challenging weather conditions for airline operations. For departing flights, the crews must be able to taxi, then see a certain distance (by counting runway lights) down the runway or be informed by ATC of the measured RVR (runway visual range). For arriving aircraft, at most airports and for the vast majority of instrument approaches, they must be able to see the runway at a certain (decision) height before continuing the approach to land or execute a missed approach if not. Forecasting precise fog conditions and trends is extremely difficult, yet the IOC, Dispatch and the operating crews all depend on a high degree of accuracy and prediction to enable the creation of accurate flight plans, sufficient carriage of fuel and timely departures. Fog can form or dissipate rapidly, changing the circumstances markedly and making operations difficult to pre-empt. Sometimes, fog is covered by cloud, obscuring the sun, which slows the process of the fog burning away.

OPERATIONAL PROCESSES

IOC response

Although fog can disrupt departures from an airport if it is sufficiently thick and there is little wind to move it, by far the main problem relates to approaches and landings. Thus, flights preparing to operate to fog-risk or fog-bound airports require careful consideration. In terms of the IOC involvement, several pieces of information are needed for the risk assessment. Some of this will be asked of the station or port itself as local knowledge is usually invaluable. The Meteorologist within the IOC plays a crucial role, as does the opinion of the Operating Captain(s).

a) What are the conditions now, and at the scheduled arrival time? (Ascertaining trends in the weather may indicate whether conditions are improving or deteriorating.)
b) Have other aircraft been landing, or are any at present?
c) Are aircraft holding at present? (This may encourage an IOC to dispatch a flight if other aircraft (or ATC) are anticipating landings in the short term.)
d) Are there other arrivals due at the same time as the flight in question? (Landings or missed approaches/diversions by other aircraft may help to inform the IOC's, and the operating crew's decisions appropriately.)
e) What is the forecast period for the fog? (If thick fog is forecast to continue for several hours with little change, a decision will be made either to hold at the departure port with a view to operating delayed or even consider the worth of operating the flight at all.)
f) How much fuel is/are the aircraft carrying? (If Controllers believe the fog will lift close to the arrival time, or that they are more willing to *hold* for a period rather than *divert* in a particular case, they may request additional fuel to be carried – this will delay the flight of course, as the refueller would probably need to be recalled to the aircraft.)
g) What alternates have been planned? (If several flights are operating to the fog-bound port, and their crews nominate the same alternate, congestion may arise at the alternate port if there are multiple diversions.)
h) How long can the aircraft hold before diverting?
i) Can the use of a different alternate increase holding time?
j) Has there been a history at that port over the last few days? If so, when did the fog dissipate previously, and were the circumstances similar to the current event?

Having gathered such information, the IOC then has options to consider:

a) The aircraft could depart (either on schedule or delayed) if there were a good chance of landing without excessive holding.
b) If other aircraft (other companies) have decided to depart according to a similar schedule, this might influence the IOC's decision. (Others might have more current information, or worse – they could be working on obsolete advice, so the rigour of the information process needs to be both comprehensive and thorough.)
c) If it departs, should it hold close to the destination for a limited time (given that fuel is expensive!) with the expectation that ATC will let it execute an approach or two?
d) If the forecast is for the fog to dissipate at some estimate after the scheduled arrival time, should the flight be delayed to coincide with this later time?
e) If the fog is not expected to change for several hours up to and beyond the arrival time, should the flight be delayed substantially, or cancelled? (Cancellation may result in a simple 'out and back' cancellation, but if the aircraft is committed to continue on to a third port, should another option be considered?)
f) If, once the fog has lifted, the airport subsequently is inundated with arrivals, can the IOC start dispatching flights, and if so, should the arrivals be staggered to even the traffic flow (and keep delays to a minimum)?

CLOUD

Cloud formation in itself is not generally a concern for operating into and out of airports, subject to the type of cloud (note that cumulonimbus or CB clouds are often associated with thunderstorms – en route and at airports – both of which are discussed below). Low cloud on the approach path may be a concern for meeting minimum conditions either for a visual or instrument approach. The IOC through its meteorological function will be alerted to conditions such as forecast low cloud, as will the operating crews of the flights.

IOC response

The circumstances are similar but not as challenging as for a fog condition. Whereas fog can be quite unpredictable, cloud formation and dissipation are less so. Often, cloud base height above the airfield fluctuates

OPERATIONAL PROCESSES

and the thinking may well be to consider dispatching a flight with sufficient fuel for holding at or near the destination airport until conditions
permit an approach and landing. Should low cloud obscure one approach
to, or one end of, the runway, subject to the wind conditions and air
traffic there may be an opportunity for an approach from the opposite
end. Sometimes ATC may instigate this or the operating crew request,
but this may also be an opportunity for astute IOC Controllers.

Information required in this instance is as follows:

a) Between the IOC (involving the Meteorology area), Operating
   Captains and perhaps the port staff, what is the perceived risk of operating on time? That is, would the aircraft be expected to land without
   too much difficulty (i.e., extensive holding or missed approaches)?
b) How much fuel is the aircraft carrying?
c) What alternates have been planned?
d) How long can the aircraft hold before diverting?

The options also are similar:

a) If the cloud base is becoming lower, what are the wind conditions
   like? Is there a chance of executing an approach from the opposite
   end (subject to instrument procedures and ATC requirements)?
b) If not, should the flight depart on schedule?
c) If the cloud base is fluctuating, should the flight depart on schedule?

The thinking processes will be informed by meteorological and ATC
advice and also take into account crew assessment of the conditions, and
local airport knowledge. The success or otherwise of recent or current
attempts to land also help to inform the picture.

WIND

Wind affects operations in several ways. In flight, strong headwinds may
add extensive time to planned flight durations. If the flight plan provides
for the forecast headwinds, then sufficient fuel for the flight (including
all necessary reserves) will be carried and the flight can operate normally.
However, if winds greatly exceed the forecast wind, an aircraft already in
flight will likely have to divert into an en-route port to uplift additional
fuel. In contrast, strong tailwinds shorten flight time, which saves time

and hence fuel (maybe even crew duty time) but brings about a different consideration. If, for example, a flight is scheduled to arrive at a port at the end of a curfew (e.g., an overnight flight scheduled to arrive at 0600), a significantly shorter flight time may mean that the flight either has to be slowed significantly (which leads to inefficiency and additional fuel burn) or as is commonly done, delayed at the departure port to avoid arriving during the curfew period.

Of more significance is the presence of strong, changeable winds, and in particular wind shear, around airports, making approaches more challenging and in some cases, dangerous. Where the runway configurations (and ATC procedures) allow, aircraft will normally take off and land into the prevailing wind. The limits applying to aircraft taking off and landing in cross-winds operations are constrained according to the aircraft manufacturer's certification. Thus, operations into single-runway airports that are experiencing strong cross-winds may not be possible. Even at large major airports, and despite normal ATC procedures enabling the use of multi-directional runways on most occasions, strong winds from a given direction may reduce the availability of some runways, thereby severely limiting traffic movements at the airport resulting in traffic build-up, congestion and delays to inbound flights.

IOC response

Cross-wind conditions are a particular cause for concern within the IOC. If adverse wind conditions at specific airports are expected to disrupt a flight for the reasons given above, the IOC together with the Pilot in Command will consider several options, each of which has a number of considerations:

a) If the strong wind conditions are likely to dissipate *before* arrival, departure should be on time.
b) If conditions are expected to persist *until* about the time of arrival, can additional fuel be uplifted to enable a period of holding?
c) What alternate(s) is nominated?
d) How much additional fuel must be carried taking into account the alternate(s) required?
e) Will this additional fuel result in a payload offload?
f) If conditions are expected to last well beyond arrival time, should the aircraft even be dispatched with little probability of being able to land? Is there another (unaffected) airport lying close to the original destination such that passengers could be road transported between the two locations?

WIND CHANGE EFFECTS

The unavailability of runways due to strong winds at a port is also a major concern for the IOC, as the level of aircraft movements (take-offs and landings) can be reduced significantly. In addition to more predictable winds and their effects, frontal systems moving through can have a significant effect on runway usage and therefore traffic patterns.

> At a major airport with two runways at right angles to each other, the level of movements was designated as 100 movements per hour, given that light and variable wind conditions enabled the use of multi-directions for operations. However, after the passage of a frontal system, the prevailing wind strengthened considerably such that only a single-runway operation became possible. Now with only one runway in use, the movement rate was reduced by some 30–40%. As low cloud on the approach required a full instrument approach procedure, the traffic flow was further reduced. This resulted in aircraft having to enter holding patterns at various points en route to the airport, and with the increase in traffic congestion, extensive holding delays began to occur. Whereas the aircraft had departed their origins with sufficient fuel to cater for the weather circumstances, the additional ATC requirements for holding patterns was far in excess of their fuel reserve capability and a number of aircraft diverted as a result. Accordingly, to mitigate the effects of both lengthy delays and the diversions, the IOC began removing a number of flights from the schedules, thereby providing buffers to help absorb the numerous disruptions.

THUNDERSTORMS

In many parts of the world (e.g., the tropics) thunderstorms can occur all year. In other regions, they are more seasonal (e.g., the USA in summer), but of course can occur at any times of the year given appropriate conditions. The nature of thunderstorms can be extremely hazardous both to aircraft in flight as well as to staff on the tarmac. Operationally, they can create turmoil for airlines. Main in-flight disturbances can include severe turbulence, damaging hail, icing, lightning strikes (which may cause minor damage or equipment failures, and often require the aircraft to undergo maintenance checking after landing) and heavy rain. But at and around airports, thunderstorms can also produce tornados, windshear and dangerous microbursts, any of which can affect aircraft taking off and landing. Therefore, crews endeavour to avoid the worst effects of these phenomena for the sake of aircraft safety and passenger comfort. So, if arriving, they will tend to be held by ATC some distance away from the field until the storms have passed or conditions are deemed safe for continuation of movements. A consequence is that this creates a significant increase in air traffic inbound for the airport as explained in the example above. In addition, departing aircraft may be held on the ground by ATC or the crews may elect to delay their departure themselves until the departure route is relatively clear.

Conditions at airports can also be hazardous. When lightning is observed within five nautical miles of an airport, a standard approach is to remove all personnel from the tarmac. In the cases in which lightning is actually striking the ground, all activities cease, to the extent that aircraft will be stopped by ATC wherever they are (even if during pushback or taxiing), and no movements (take-offs or landings) will be permitted. As thunderstorms pass over an airport, conditions on the ground can fluctuate considerably. Winds can change direction and speed abruptly, which can affect runway usage and therefore approach directions and procedures. In some cases, the severity of the weather results in surface winds of a particular strength and direction, but immediately above (say, 1000 ft), the wind could be the opposite direction with far stronger force. This creates havoc for approaches and landings, and often results in missed approaches (go-rounds), which exacerbates the queue of aircraft waiting to land (and take off) and contributes to inevitable diversions.

IOC response

The duration of a thunderstorm is usually from 20 minutes to 1½ hours (for airmass thunderstorms) or several hours (for multi-cell, steady state thunderstorms). More often than not, most flights will operate with the expectation that perhaps after some delay incorporating holding patterns near the destination, landings are probable. Thus, the first IOC response is to gather some information:

a) What times are thunderstorms predicted at the airport?
b) How long are they expected to last? (This can influence a decision to delay departure.)
c) How many aircraft are due to arrive? (If a high number, air traffic holding and congestion are likely to impact further on the schedule.)

d) What alternate(s) is/are nominated?
e) How long can the aircraft hold before diverting to the alternate? (With thunderstorms passing through an airport, the expectation is that perhaps after some minor holding, there is a strong probability of landing.)

The options include the following:

a) The most likely action is to dispatch the aircraft on schedule with sufficient fuel to hold (based on the forecast) for an expected period, using the nominated alternate(s) in case of diversion. This may necessitate offloading payload to accommodate the fuel required.
b) Sometimes, if storm activity is severe and of extended duration, an option may be to hold an aircraft on the ground at the originating port. This is a viable option in the operation of a very short-haul sector, when it is dictated by available slot times, or it is known that traffic build-up at the affected airport is likely to exacerbate holding times considerably.

COLD CONDITIONS – SNOW AND ICE

Inclement weather such as heavy snow and icing conditions require specific activity in relation to airport performance and aircraft preparation. Airports located in prone areas are typically well equipped with snow ploughs and other heavy machinery designed to rapidly remove contamination from movement areas. On occasions though, conditions such as heavy snow create significant disruption as the capability of equipment is exceeded. Other than complete airport closures, most disruptive during these events is the extent of delays due to the need for de-icing aircraft. This is a process either performed at a number of de-icing stations (most often de-icing pads) around the airport, or carried out with mobile equipment at the gate. However, there are only a certain number of de-icing pads and limited equipment and staff. There is also a limited time that the spray or other treatment is effective, so de-icing is required as close to the expected departure time as possible. As a result, demand is usually high at busy times and delays are inevitable as the queue of aircraft needing the service grows.

IOC response

The IOC generally has a number of considerations to weigh up in terms of departing traffic:

a) The duration, extent and severity of the storm.
b) The level of traffic on the ground building up and requiring de-icing treatment.
c) The capacity and resources of the various de-icing systems in place (and hence calculated waiting time).
d) If the storm is particularly severe, the IOC will seek information from the Station Manager or Port Coordinator as to the capability of the infrastructure between city and airport so as to enable customer (and crew) transport to and from the terminal precinct.

The options include the following:

a) If de-icing facilities are in high demand with imminent disruption to several services, IOCs may select specific operations to be prioritised with others either delayed or cancelled in order to protect the greater network.
b) If a snowstorm is particularly severe and expected to be long-lasting, the IOC may elect to suspend *all operations* into that airport for a period.

HOT CONDITIONS – HIGH TEMPERATURE

Conditions at some airports located in deserts, some equatorial locations or regions prone to extreme weather, can result in very high temperatures. With reduced air density, aircraft take-off and climb performance may be substantially compromised, limiting the payload and/or range of the aircraft.

IOC response

To an extent, planning several days ahead of the day of operations tends to reveal operational problems such as this and steps can be taken well ahead to distribute the load onto other flights or change the routing of the flight to enable an en-route 'technical' stop for fuel. In some cases involving long-haul flights operating from known high-temperature airports, the Commercial department may have limited the saleable payload by blocking out a number of seats on the aircraft. This artificially limits the maximum weight of the aircraft and avoids offloading any payload. However, on the day of operation, temperatures can exceed forecasts such that a weight or performance problem only becomes known when the flight plan is prepared or even later, once the crew have signed on and considered all the information at hand. Then the decision to manage the problem falls to the IOC.

TIDAL MOVEMENT

A quite unusual circumstance is the operation of an RPT service into an airport that uses a beach surface for taking off and landing. This can only occur, of course, at low tide when the beach is relatively dry and firm, and when general weather conditions enable the service to operate. From a scheduling perspective, the timetabled arrival and departure times must be planned in advance according to tide movements.

IOC response

For the IOC, the flights are expected to operate within the known tidal conditions. Should weather conditions or surface conditions at the airport not be conducive to operating, or should other reasons (e.g., maintenance, crewing) prevent a timely operation, the IOC will seek to delay or cancel the flight(s) until the conditions above are suitable, which may imply the same or similar time the following day. The decisions are more or less straightforward in such cases, and a lot of reliance is placed on the advice from the aircraft's Captain, any qualified meteorological personnel, as well as the staff located at the particular airport.

TYPHOON/CYCLONE/HURRICANE

The occurrence of a typhoon (cyclone or hurricane, terminology subject to the region of the world) is of major significance to an airline and is the cause of massive disruption in and around the affected ports. To give this event due attention, a worked example is provided in some detail toward the end of this chapter.

ENGINEERING

Disruptions due to maintenance (or technical) problems are an everyday occurrence in an airline operation. There are numerous reasons of

OPERATIONAL PROCESSES

course – from a broken tray table to an engine change, but whatever the problem, each has the potential to disrupt a flight. Most commonly, disruptions occur during service; that is while the aircraft is engaged in scheduled activities. Unserviceabilities may be discovered while undertaking ground inspections during turnarounds between flights, or componentry may fail during any stage of the flight. Aircraft may be grounded and require Engineers and parts before being permitted to continue, or may be cleared to fly with some performance limitation or other restriction. Aircraft can also arrive on the line (at the gate) late after overnight work, can be damaged during handling or ground servicing, by passengers (on-board breakages), or by weather (e.g., hail damage or lightning strikes) and so forth.

IOC response

Maintenance disruptions can be another area of significant challenge in the IOC. Timely and appropriate engineering advice is crucial to identifying and assessing a problem, and then determining the most efficient course of action to return the aircraft to service. The difficulty for IOCs lies in taking the expert advice on the one hand, while on the other, determining how best to deliver schedule recovery to customers. Depending on all the circumstances of the maintenance issue (and other variances), the IOC will require some or all of the following information:

a) What exactly is wrong with the aircraft? (Initially this may be hard to determine without due expert input.)
b) Where has the initial advice come from? (This is a most important clarification, as early advice may often be communicated by a well-meaning but innocent third party, with little or no engineering knowledge.)
c) Are licensed Engineers (appropriate for the problem) available to assess?
d) Can they fix the aircraft?
e) Do they *need* to fix the aircraft (i.e., can it operate on an MEL? This may be possible with a speed or height limitation for example – advice from Engineering will lead this discussion.)
f) What is the ETS (estimated time of serviceability)? (This provides the first guide (though perhaps crude at an early stage) for the IOC to start gauging the impact and enable a recovery option to begin.)
g) Are there parts available at this port?
h) Do other airlines have a part that can be used?

OPERATIONAL PROCESSES

i) Are parts and Engineers required to be positioned from another port? (In this case, the aircraft becomes AOG (aircraft on ground), i.e., grounded until rectified.)
j) Is the weather conducive to fixing the aircraft on the ramp, or does it need to be towed to a hangar?

Another set of questions addresses different issues, subject to the time of the unserviceability in relation to the scheduled departure time.

a) Are the passengers on board? (If the advice received is that passengers are not being boarded, or are being disembarked, the expectation is that a lengthy delay is quite likely.)
b) When did the crews (both the Pilots and Flight Attendants) sign on?
c) What is the latest sign-off time for these crews?
d) If the delay becomes quite protracted, are there replacement crews that could be used?

Quite specific customer-related considerations also need to be addressed.

a) Working with the CJM team, are there VIPs/CIPs on board? (The CJM team can then assume responsibility for managing this.)
b) What time limitations (normally set by government legislation) apply to the customers remaining on board an aircraft? (After a certain time, legislation may require airlines to de-board an aircraft.)
c) Are there customs and immigration facilities available to process customers if de-boarding is required? (This might arise if an aircraft has diverted into a port due to some maintenance issue.)
d) Is the airport infrastructure able to cope should customers de-board? (Is there accommodation, transport, food outlets?)
e) Are there any *special needs* customers requiring appropriate attention?
f) Are there any unaccompanied minors (who will need appropriate staff supervision/accompaniment) on board?
g) Are there any specific freight uplift requirements (e.g. requiring special containment, handling or storage)?

With this information gathered (and keeping in mind that circumstances change, information is updated, and new advice may then alter the state of the problem), the IOC can start to consider options:

a) If the parts are available and the Engineers can fix the aircraft, an initial ETD (estimated time of departure) may be set for the flight.

OPERATIONAL PROCESSES

Nowadays, the digital communications update various airport and other displays as well as passenger hand-held devices, so committing to such times has to reflect a realistic estimate. One difficulty is the opportunity cost that may exist if, having set an ETD, the aircraft becomes serviceable earlier than expected. Either the time would have to be revised to an *earlier* departure which may be extremely difficult to achieve, or the later ETD has to be respected, with due wastage. This is why an accurate ETS from Engineering is so essential before any advice goes out to the customers. It is also the reason that conservative ETDs are set and may become rolling should rectification take increasingly longer times. In conjunction with Engineering, ideally the aim with regard to an engineering delay is to achieve the published ETS. Timing is crucial to avoid misleading the customers. *Underestimating* the time and continual revisions result in rolling delays, while *overestimating* the time wastes opportunities to minimise the disruption.

b) Can the problem be isolated to this one flight or at least a small number of flights?
c) Can an aircraft swap or some alternative action protect other flights?
d) Is there any threat to curfew and, if so, can this be eliminated through similar protection strategies?
e) Is there any problem renegotiating new slot times?
f) If there are no parts (or licensed Engineers) available and the aircraft becomes AOG, should the flight be delayed or cancelled (if cancelled, what is the best option to accommodate customers on alternate services, either with this airline or with others)?

AIR TRAFFIC

Air traffic delays are typically consequences of other problems such as weather or congestion both on the ground and in the air. Programs such as ground stops or the invoking of slot times if not already in place, alleviate some of this congestion by providing an orderly flow of traffic (albeit with delays) in and out of airports. There may be other problems such as systems failures, navigational aid failures or out of service conditions, power failures, or communications issues but mostly these are uncommon. In some airports, the loss of a high-speed taxiway (enabling aircraft to exit a runway expeditiously) due to works, for example, may result in longer runway dwell times as aircraft slow to turn off the runway at a suitable exit point, with a consequential reduction in the rate of approaches being conducted. In the event of an aircraft becoming disabled on a runway (e.g., due to a burst tyre or loss of steering) this is likely to close the runway until removal can be effected. In a single-runway port, a lengthy removal process may well result in diversions as inbound aircraft will not normally be carrying additional fuel to hold for very long (other than mandatory reserves). Increasingly of concern are airspace closures due to industrial, staffing, military needs, or due to political tension and areas of conflict.

IOC response

The IOC response will depend on the causal factors and the extent of ATC delays. Usually, problems caused by weather and congestion will become evident quickly as delays begin to emerge and revised slot times advised. IOC responses may initially follow a somewhat predictable pattern of sourcing information:

a) What aircraft are being delayed inbound and for how long?
b) How much fuel is each aircraft carrying?
c) What alternates have they each nominated?
d) How are the alternates coordinated so as to prevent traffic congestion and/or overwhelming the resources at any particular alternate(s)?
e) How long can each hold before diverting?
f) What aircraft are being held on the ground?
g) Have these aircraft sufficient fuel on board or do they need additional fuel to enable holding given the circumstances?

The IOC actions regarding the above information are likely to be similar to the responses in weather situations, and therefore are not repeated here. However, in the case of a runway closure, the IOC will need specific information:

a) What are the circumstances of the disabled aircraft?
b) How long is the runway expected to stay closed?
c) What aircraft are holding at present?
d) What other aircraft are due to arrive?
e) How much fuel and holding do these aircraft have?
f) What aircraft are due to depart?
g) Will they be disrupted, and if so, to what extent?

OPERATIONAL PROCESSES

Subject to these answers, the time of day and other circumstances, further considerations such as proximity to curfews, crew hours limitations, connecting flights, and so forth may also be of relevance. Based on the information gleaned through this process, the IOC can then establish a course of action.

a) Should the disabled aircraft occupy the only runway available and the expectation is that removal will take considerable time, the IOC would normally wish for inbound aircraft to hold as long as practicable as long as there is a strong likelihood of landing.
b) However, unless these flights are carrying sufficient fuel to hold for extended periods (unlikely if they are only carrying standard fuel reserves) they will most probably divert promptly, unless the problem is very short term. The IOC then will probably elect to have the aircraft refuelled and sent back as soon as it is evident that a landing can be accomplished.

CREWING

Disruption due to crew-related issues can be caused by reaching duty hours limitations, crew sickness or fatigue, crew rest requirements or exceptional circumstances such as this example below:

At a destination airport, a technical crew operated a smaller version of a particular type of aircraft one evening, and then took crew rest, as planned. (The crew from the previous day operated the aircraft out.) When the crew signed on the next day to take the flight back to the hub, they found that the airline had upgraded the aircraft to a larger model of the same type. While licensed to fly the larger version, they were not endorsed to taxi and turn the larger aircraft at one end of the runway at this particular airport, rendering the crew unable to operate the flight, and requiring the airline to position another crew to that port, resulting in a lengthy delay.

Crew sickness at a crewing base is not normally disruptive due to (a) reserves who may be on duty at the airport and available to fly immediately, or (b) other reserve crews who are not at the airport but are 'on call'. However, crew sickness at an 'out station' where back-up crews are not resident, is more troublesome and calls for alternative action. The IOC will seek to establish the following:

a) Is there a replacement crew at this port? (sometimes there may be a crew taking crew rest for a number of days, who could be called to operate an earlier than planned flight). Considerations are whether they have had the legal rest period, and whether they have consumed any alcohol within the legally permitted time prior to a duty period. Sometimes, a more expeditious solution may be to wait for the original crew members to recover and present fit for flying (of course, this is dependent upon the nature of the problem).

b) If there is no crew at this port, is there one at a nearby port who could be positioned (dead-head) to operate? Achieving the intended flight schedule may be possible providing the total duty time (including positioning) is within limits. If the replacement crew have to take additional rest, little may be gained. Perhaps, though, achieving some of the schedule is possible by operating into a midway port en route, and thus reducing the duty time. Of course, there needs to be a replacement crew sent out to this port to continue the flight.

IOC response

IOC strategies can be quite novel at certain times to recover from a crew-related disruption. In the case of pilots' ToD limits for long-haul operations there are a number of options that may be invoked.

a) If a ToD with *two pilots* is the limiting factor, can the ToD be increased by adding an additional Pilot for the flight, or can the ToD be reduced by operating via an interim port and replacing the original crew members?

b) If the Captain (or Aircraft Commander in some airlines) becomes ill, the flight cannot operate without another Captain, but if a First Officer has reported ill, consideration is given as to whether another Captain can replace the First Officer (i.e., have two Captains operating, although only one is the nominated Pilot in Command). If this is possible, the 'fill-in' Captain must be right-hand seat endorsed. Of course, any plan that robs resources earlier than planned, needs to cover these subsequently, so there is a knock-on effect.

OPERATIONAL PROCESSES

In the case of long-haul operations with heavy or augmented crew complements (i.e., three or four flight crew members), other options come into play:

c) If the flight plan can be shortened (i.e., more direct routing), the ToD time may be reduced to an extent that a three-crew complement can be used instead of the rostered four-crew complement.
d) One way to shorten a flight is to cruise at a slightly higher speed, which may satisfy the ToD limit, but may require an increase in fuel uplift and will certainly raise the cost factor of the flight.

Cabin crew

There is a legal requirement for a minimum number of cabin crew due to the need to provide safety on board and, in particular, to operate exit doors and evacuate passengers in an emergency. Often, airlines may carry additional crew members over and above this legal requirement. This comes at a cost of course, but the rationale is to provide additional levels of service, especially for premium class travellers. In the case of a shortage of cabin crew (e.g., due to sickness), there are a number of strategies that can be employed to overcome the shortage.

a) Dispensation to operate with reduced crew (this will probably need agreement from both the union (if applicable) and Customer Service Manager/Director – the Senior Flight Attendant on board) but must still meet regulatory requirements. (All doors must be staffed for evacuation considerations, but service levels may be slightly diminished.)
b) Restricting the passenger load (the ratio of Flight Attendants to customers varies from airline to airline, but the regulatory requirements must still be met).
c) If an augmented technical crew (i.e. three or four pilots) is operating the flight, the most junior Pilot (e.g., Second Officer) could be stationed at one of the doors just for take-off and landing.

AIRPORT

The airports can be a source of disruption despite the meticulous planning and preparation that occurs prior to the day of operation. In terms of the overall operation, an airport serves as a filter for the IOC.

OPERATIONAL PROCESSES

It has its own issues and deals with these under its own jurisdiction. It is only when a system failure or an event occurs that extends beyond the control of the airport and affects the schedule that the IOC may become involved. Some airport disruptions are the result of unserviceabilities or unavailability of equipment, including but not limited to the following:

a) Runways, taxiways (due to works, or damage) or apron parking areas.
b) Navigational aids, airfield lighting, weather monitoring equipment (in and around the immediate airport vicinity).
c) ATC communications and equipment (e.g., radar).
d) Aviation rescue and fire fighting (ARFF). The explanation of the categorisation system for this service is beyond this text, but suffice it to say that the amount of equipment, level of serviceability and the capability of the service can affect aircraft operations through an airport.
e) Aerobridges, nose in guidance systems.
f) Fuel issues (hydrant fuel systems or tanker availability), off specification fuel, fuel supply shortages.
g) Terminal check-in systems, baggage belt systems.
h) Power failures (affecting systems as shown above, but also the airport's fuel pumping capability).
i) Damage as a result of fire or storm activity (e.g., roof leakages or collapses, flooding).

Other more uncommon airport-related disruptions may be caused by procedural issues, human error in service provision, or other factors:

a) Airspace closures or restrictions at or near an airport due to an air-show or similar event (air-shows usually provide for scheduled arrivals and departures within the show agenda but other restrictions may occur).
b) Bay or gate availability and planning issues. Bay planning can be problematic especially in the case of a limited number of available gates to use, that also accommodate the dimensions of the aircraft. Certain gates may be required for wide-body aircraft, or those exceeding specific wing spans, lengths, or weights, and adjacent gates may or may not be appropriate for two wide-body aircraft due to their wing span. Bay planning needs to take into account commonly scheduled movements (e.g., two departures at once) to avoid multiple pushbacks in adjacent or nearby bays, for example. In addition, positioning of connecting flights in close proximity to each other serves to expedite

OPERATIONAL PROCESSES

passenger flow in the terminal and assist in transhipping baggage and freight on the tarmac.

c) Human error can surface in a number of ways such as:

    i. incorrectly fuelled aircraft (usually requiring recall of the fueller with subsequent delays)

    ii. catering placed on incorrect aircraft (possibly delaying both flights)

    iii. incorrect or incomplete loading of aircraft (e.g., leaving baggage unloaded)

    iv. incorrect or incomplete paperwork.

d) Third-party handling issues (e.g., not performing up to contracted levels).

e) Aerobridge manoeuvring or ground service equipment vehicles causing damage to aircraft.

f) Congestion in terminal security processing, customs or check-in areas.

g) Demonstrations, protests.

IOC response

Airport-initiated disruptions are advised to the IOC through the airline's Airport Station Manager or Port Coordinator. This position, being local, usually has the clearest and most updated information as to the particular problem. Therefore, advice as to the duration or extensiveness of a disruption will be instigated here. The IOC treats these problems as for most others, seeking information as to the potential impact on arrivals and departures or other impacts on the airline (e.g., affecting its brand), and gauging the impact on immediate and consequential services.

CUSTOMERS

Customers themselves can cause significant operational disruptions by failing to check-in, arriving late at a gate-lounge, or failing to board at the nominated times. They may also present at the boarding gate in an unfit state (e.g., affected by alcohol). If this is detected by gate boarding staff or the cabin crew on board the aircraft, the customers are usually denied travel, and due to the security requirements to keep customers and their baggage together, this will often result in having to identify, locate and remove the baggage from the aircraft's hold, typically causing

OPERATIONAL PROCESSES

a considerable delay. With online check-in now normalised, the physical whereabouts of customers is largely unknown by airport staff. Whereas in earlier days, check-in at the airport guaranteed their presence at least within a small distance of the gate and within earshot of announcements, this is not the case today. Smart device and airport concession visitations may contribute to some levels of tracking inside the terminal, but late or no-show customers who have otherwise checked in, but been caught up in some transport issue on the way to the airport may be an unknown quantity.

IOC response

Delays caused by customer issues in the terminal are normally managed by the airport staff with updates provided to the IOC at regular intervals or on request. Only if the delays are expected to become significant will a decision be sought from the IOC. In the case of spurious check-in information, whereby it is not known how many customers are actually within the airport terminal in time for flights, perhaps due to some transport or access problem, the IOC will rely on the information provided, again, by the airline's Airport Station Manager or Port Coordinator. Questions that need to be asked of them will include the following:

a) What sort of transport (or other) issue is taking place?
b) What is the expected duration of the situation?
c) Which flights are affected?
d) How many customers are actually at the airport now?

With this information, options to be considered include the following:

a) If an accident has blocked a major access route into the airport such that very few customers have arrived at the airport, an assessment of departing flights is made to establish which flights can be held and for how long, without impinging on successive schedules.
b) If the vast majority of customers are believed to be at the airport, flights are likely to be sent, with any late customers accommodated on later services. This then becomes the role of the CJM team.
c) If the utilisation is extremely tight with little leeway available for delaying the initial flights, they may be dispatched with only partial loads, in order to protect the network.

OPERATIONAL PROCESSES

INDUSTRIAL

Delays of an industrial nature vary from black-bans, work-to-rules campaigns, stop-work meetings, short strike action or significant strike actions. Known industrial issues whereby airlines are advised of impending action (e.g., by ATC, fuellers, baggage handlers, and so forth) can largely be planned for, ahead of time. As a result, the day of operation typically reflects a diminished schedule as the commercial changes to fit flights around the issue are normally made prior. Thus, the IOC manages this reduced schedule similar to normal operating days. However, when sudden industrial action is taken, such as an instant stop-work or strike action, the resulting disruptions become significant.

IOC response

Responses to industrial activity vary enormously as the industrial climate can fluctuate from being insignificant to highly volatile, necessitating quite distinct actions. Known industrial action plans such as stop-work meetings say from 1000–1400 on a future date, will have been allowed prior to the current day. That is, schedule adjustments will already have been adapted around the disruption. However, industrial action on the day of operation (e.g., withdrawal of labour) can be highly disruptive. The IOC's response is governed by the 'rules' set by the industrial body. Subject to preceding or current negotiation between the company and the industrial organisation, a resolution may be found, with the result that delays and cancellations are minimised. On other occasions, the action is protracted with little immediate recourse, resulting in far more convoluted remedies.

COMMERCIAL

During the operating day, there may be ad-hoc requests for commercial reasons (e.g., additional capacity, or a request for a charter). This may require additional flying (if extra flights can satisfy the need) or a process of upgrading/downgrading of aircraft types to provide the extra seats or cargo capacity. For example, if additional capacity were needed to serve the ports A and B, and flights operating the routes A-C-A only justified a smaller aircraft, the IOC may consider substituting a wide-body aircraft

126

in lieu of a narrow-body aircraft (upgrading) A-B-A, and a narrow-body aircraft in lieu of a wide-body aircraft (downgrading) A-C-A.

IOC response

The request in the IOC will usually emanate from its Commercial function. If the request is for additional flights on the day of operation, the procedure would entail searching for an available aircraft (of appropriate size), technical and cabin crews, and ensuring airport handling and slot availability can be managed. In the case of substituting aircraft within the existing schedules, juggling of the aircraft patterns without compromising other flights may be the most difficult component, especially if aircraft patterns remain out of position overnight. In addition, upgrading and downgrading flights will usually have implications for both technical and cabin crewing areas.

SECURITY

Disruptions due to security can range from concerns inside the terminal building (e.g., security screening process) to on-board incidents and other threats against the airline and/or its customers or staff. In many cases, and indeed the most serious events, the airline's Security Department in conjunction with State authorities (e.g., governments) manage the process, with advice to the IOC as to the status and developments as they become known. Through monitoring of current world events, the security function within the IOC may also be the information channel with regard to advice about overflight issues, current or potential military activity, or specific threats to airports or the airline itself. More common events involve terminal security processes. If security is believed to have been compromised (e.g., a need to clarify or re-confirm passenger security compliance, on some rare occasions not only passengers but *all individuals* within the sterile part of the terminal may need to be ejected entirely from the terminal and completely rescreened. This may quickly become a dramatic and somewhat chaotic process of having to evacuate all personnel from the immediate terminal (i.e., building complex) as well as those who have already boarded aircraft and may otherwise be ready for departure. As can be imagined, the extent of turmoil caused rapidly influences all departures for several hours, thereby causing widespread disruption for all affected airlines using that part (or all) of the terminal.

IOC response

In the case of a terminal evacuation and subsequent re-screening of all personnel, the IOC will be guided by the airport as to the expected duration, flights impacted, and size of delays. This information will help to inform the likely network effects, to which can be added the impact on the fleet utilisation, crews and tranships, and of course, taking into account the time of day, may also impact on curfews or other limiting factors. As a result, the IOC may need to select immediate and ongoing flights that may be delayed, as well as identifying where potential cancellations may be made that will assist in restoring the schedules as best as possible.

MISCELLANEOUS

Of course, there are numerous miscellaneous incidents that may occur that are largely outside the control of the airline, including such events as earthquakes, tsunamis and sudden volcanic eruptions, for example. Each of these is handled on its merits. However, as has been observed in various parts of the world, the incidences of volcanic disturbances can be far reaching with quite devastating consequences should the ash cloud be extensive.

IOC response

In these types of events, world organisations, various governments and senior airline management become involved. In turn, the IOC will respond as these bodies determine.

WORKED EXAMPLE

The following example describes the initiation, development, approach and impact of a major weather phenomenon, and outlines some of the thought processes that underpin procedures and strategies undertaken within the IOC leading up to and during the event. In this scenario, the advice to the IOC applies either to the Duty Manager or Controller (or Dispatcher), but for simplicity of expression, the reference will be just to the 'IOC'.

Example scenario – forming typhoon (day of operation minus 4)

The Meteorologist attached to the IOC has been made aware by the Regional Specialised Meteorological Centre (RSMC) in Tokyo of a tropical storm developing about 150 kilometres off the south-east coast of Japan. Currently the storm is moving slowly north-west, and at present not demanding any more than just an awareness and monitoring of it. The Meteorologist will continue to scan various sources of information including government sites and weather channels on world news stations and may also be in contact with the US Joint Typhoon Warning Centre (JTWC) or other authorities.

1st advice to the IOC
The advice to the IOC may be of an alert nature only, just to make the staff aware of the presence of a potential weather situation.

IOC reasoning
The IOC would be aware that tropical storms such as this are common in this area and especially for a particular seasonal period (e.g., typhoon season). Until there is a development, there is little point devoting resources at this stage. Tropical storms may intensify, track in several directions, and eventually have some operational impact, but also they may weaken and dissipate.

IOC action
No action is needed at this stage. It is a matter only of being made aware. If a status board exists within the IOC, some notation may be added as a preliminary brief to relevant staff. No concern for schedules is merited yet.

Situation update – forming typhoon (day of operation minus 3)

The tropical storm has deepened and intensified over the past 24 hours, with wind speeds now in excess of 60 knots, and accordingly has now been classified as a severe tropical storm. The system continues to move north-west and is expected to intensify into a typhoon within 12–15 hours. The Meteorologists have begun to employ software to plot the movement and project the track over the next 24 or so hours.

OPERATIONAL PROCESSES

2nd advice to the IOC

As the severe storm is expected to form into a typhoon, the Meteorologist now alerts the IOC to the changing weather pattern. Any information such as a map with track projections and possible crossings of the coast may be worthwhile.

IOC reasoning

From an initial briefing, this heightened state of awareness starts a process in train whereby the IOC starts to consider whether this situation is likely to have any impact on the operations. Much of the thought processes will be influenced by Controllers' previous experience in dealing with major weather disturbances. As the IOC is likely to have control of the next 5–7 days' flying patterns, attention may now be drawn to the IOC planning function which is responsible for examining potential operational or commercial threats to the schedule. Although the typhoon is away from the coast, tracks of flight paths in close proximity to the storm will be considered and, if necessary, alternative planned tracks will be calculated to avoid the area.

IOC action

In consultation with the Meteorologist, the planner will consider the next few days' schedules in terms of aircraft and crew commitments, and the booked passenger loadings of all flights likely to be affected. Briefings will extend to senior management to forewarn of potential impact in the region as well as the key functional areas within the IOC. With the customer well and truly at the forefront of thinking, the involvement of CJM staff at this early stage is vital in considering the effects to customers of delays and possibly cancelled services to the affected ports.

Situation update – forming typhoon (day of operation minus 2)

The severe tropical storm has again intensified with sustained winds exceeding 80 knots. This is now a formidable system, and accordingly been re-classified into a typhoon. It has begun to follow a recurving path and projected to track directly toward Tokyo at an increased speed. With further intensification as it draws water from the Pacific, and barring unforeseen changes, there is a high degree of confidence that it will cross the coast within 30–36 hours. Once it crosses the coast, the sustained effects of very strong winds, very heavy rain, and flooding are expected to be significant.

3rd advice to the IOC

The Meteorologist is now in a position to provide a fully informed opinion, an accurate assessment of the path and likely impact of the impending system.

The brief to the IOC changes from a message of alert, to a status of operational risk for the IOC to consider.

IOC reasoning

The thinking now is to conduct a full risk assessment of the event. To do this, it will consider what options may be available in the event of the typhoon creating disruption and monitoring the track of the storm will largely determine the most likely course of action. The IOC team will develop a number of scenarios which can be instigated accordingly. These could include the following:

a) Option one might be to operate the normal schedule into Tokyo provided the operation is deemed safe. To consider this, advice is sought from a range of key personnel. The group could consist of a Senior Captain, the IOC Manager, the IOC Meteorologist, and Dispatch Manager, for example, and is tasked with risk assessing the situation and deciding whether it is safe to operate or not. Flight Planning/Dispatch will have already nominated diversionary airports should at any stage a decision be made not to continue to Tokyo. Considerations include the safe operation of the aircraft, in terms of potential damage, possible airport damage and access to facilities, safety and comfort for passengers on the aircraft, those on the ground and in transit to the airport, and those already at the airport (for the outbound trip).

b) Option two might be to operate to nearby airports in Japan which are unaffected or are out of the pathway of the typhoon. Considerations include operation to a non-airline port with the need for handling the aircraft to be arranged. Of course, customers would need to be transported by road/rail each way, provided the transport system is available. In addition, to operate the aircraft into a non-airline port there must also be a way to get new crews to the aircraft under the same conditions. There is also not likely to be engineering support, unless there is an arrangement with contracted staff.

c) Option three might be to delay operations into the Tokyo region until the typhoon has passed and the airport is capable of handling movements again (i.e., any damage repaired, facilities serviceable including runways, aprons, terminals, ATC and navigational aids, etc., and access roads open).

d) Option four might be to cancel the operation outright. In such a case, the next scheduled operation will be of concern. If the schedule provides for a daily operation, then the risk assessment will extend across several days. If, however, the schedule is of a less frequent operation, the cancellation isolates the extent of the disruption, and future services would then be considered on their own merit.

> The considerations will amount to a combination of what plan works in terms of aircraft utilisation, the Pilot and cabin crews concerned, and any other operational factors, and of course what is the best recovery strategy for customers. No operation will be deployed unless it is safe to do so. Further considerations must include the health and safety of the workforces in the airports themselves.
>
> **IOC action**
>
> Given the sources of information provided, and the growing expectation of disruption, the main task of the IOC will be to develop and weigh up each contingency plan to cover the likely scenarios, discussing each with the key stakeholders such as Corporate Management, Crewing Management, Engineering, Airports, Flight Operations, Commercial and CJM teams. Notably, differing approaches may be adopted subject to the characteristics of the airline. For a national carrier with multiple operations into a hub structure, cancelling or diverting services may be quite acceptable, knowing that plentiful recovery options are available. However, for a foreign carrier, the decision to cancel may not be so straightforward. Using a collaborative approach, a recommended option will be agreed and actioned subject to updated information and time scale. Again though, the need for operational autonomy within the IOC is critical to provide clear and positive direction. Consensus reached by a committee approach is distractive to the process and may not necessarily support the oversight needed and already provided by the IOC. Hence, the deliberation may end up less consultative and more decisive. Once established, this contingency plan is then transmitted to all concerned to ensure continuity and complete understanding by all parties. In this way, the IOC is fully prepared.

IMMINENT DISRUPTIONS

Within a shorter time-frame but still enabling pre-emptive actions are the more imminent disruptive events such as, for example, current weather activity likely to cause extensive delays, diversions and cancellations, or a medical event on an aircraft that also may call for a diversion for immediate attention, or an intrusion into crew rest hours with a consequential schedule delay the following day. In the case of both potential and imminent disruptions, the IOC will expend considerable effort in the hope of overcoming the disruptive effects of such events.

OPERATIONAL PROCESSES

Example scenario – imminent typhoon (day of operation minus 1)

The typhoon has intensified again and is now expected to cross the coast within 24–30 hours just south of Tokyo and tracking north-west. Expectations are much the same as the previous update, and warnings are now public as damaging winds, torrential rain and severe flooding are predicted to affect the region and of course airports.

4th advice to the IOC

The advice to the IOC now is one of imminent risk, advising of likely impact to the region, and expected duration of the typhoon.

IOC reasoning

With this development (much as expected), and input from the stakeholders, the IOC is in a sound position to select a strategy. The options may be visited again, but it is quite likely that an optimum strategy will already have been chosen and the pros and cons debated.

IOC action

Given the latest information, the IOC would probably decide to delay the whole operation into Tokyo until the typhoon has passed and any damage assessed. This will come as no shock to customers who will have been advised ahead of time. The subsequent impact on successive schedules will have been mitigated and the disruption contained within the immediate region and event.

MEASURING THE EFFECTIVENESS OF THE IOC

Given the nature of airline operations and outputs affecting thousands of customers, staff and external stakeholders, and the extensiveness and expense of resource use, systems need to be in place to measure the effectiveness of operational performance. Various measures may relate to functions associated with operations such as passenger check-in efficiency, airport gate performance, mishandled passengers and baggage, aircraft turn times, efficiency of ground-handling services and aircraft dispatch reliability. But the performance within the IOC may also be captured in a number of ways. Airline policies may well dictate the extent to which specific objectives need to be met. For example, OTP (which implies departures, but really incorporates arrivals as well) is a prime measure of the airline's operational performance, and the IOC contributes to this function through its decision processes.

It is important to point out that while 100% OTP may be desirable, a result of 50% on a highly disruptive day with numerous cancellations, diversions and delays may in fact be a satisfactory result for an IOC. Data regarding OTP are generally gathered by government instrumentalities and/or commercial and research-based organisations, and are usually available publicly, which enables comparisons to be made between carriers and may therefore influence customer preferences. The information may contain metrics for the number of flights delayed across a network, by city-pairs, or otherwise, in terms of numbers of flights and time delayed. International standards allow for 15 minutes grace before a flight is deemed to be delayed. Another form of measurement may be the level of flight cancellations. This is typically a function of the disruptors such as weather, mechanical, ATC and many other issues. Built into these data will be associated costs, both in terms of monetary and loyalty factors, but of course airlines with high levels of cancellation often are the target of the media.

NOTES

1 Van Vliet, V. 2012. Henry Gantt. Retrieved 17/09/19 from ToolsHero: www.toolshero.com/toolsheroes/henry-Gantt/
2 Stecher, D. 2018. IBS Corporate Blog: Airline Operations: What should replace the legacy systems? Retrieved 13/10/19. https://blog.ibsplc.com/airline-operations/airline-operations-what-should-replace-the-legacy-systems
3 For a more complete description of disruption strategies, see Bruce, P. 2018. Operational disruptions: causes, strategies, and consequences, in P.J. Bruce, Y. Gao and J.M.C. King (eds) *Airline Operations: A practical guide*, Abingdon, Routledge, pp. 335–339.

Part II

OPERATIONAL CONTROL IN PRACTICE

INTRODUCTION

In Part I of this book, the focus was on providing the background to the IOC, the considerations behind planning and preparing for the operating day, the nature of regular and irregular operations and, of course, the people involved in running the centre. What is often under-appreciated or completely misunderstood is the level of intensity that typifies operational activity and the thinking processes that underpin problem-solving and decision-making processes.

The intention for Part II is to demonstrate how Controllers (and Dispatchers) in an IOC actually go about this process. Thus, the focus of the scenario chapters is to demonstrate the ways in which Controllers manage problems, offering an insight into the thought processes that might occur, how and why Controllers gather specific intelligence, discerning relevant from erroneous information, how they create options and then select one over another as the preferred solution to a problem. This level of knowledge is hard to locate, being difficult to capture and even more difficult to portray in terms of assisting others learning the task. Identifying a problem and its factors, and listing options and ideal solutions, is relatively straightforward. However, having an inkling into the mindset of the more experienced Controllers is the key to accessing this level of thinking.

The first of these chapters aims to bridge the gap between Part I descriptions and Part II scenarios, providing some clarity about the depth of communication and interactivity that typically takes place during disruptions. The following three chapters detail the high-level information gathering, thought processes, and action steps taken within the IOC in terms of disruption management.

OPERATIONAL CONTROL IN PRACTICE

Chapters 6 and 7 explore IOC processes with regard to two weather disruptions, while Chapter 8 demonstrates similar processes in an engineering disruption. These three chapters use anecdotally based scenarios to replicate representative operational situations, with explicit commentary complete with depictions of activity displayed on a series of progressive Gantt charts to help explain the ways in which the IOC manages each situation. To assist the reader to follow the scenario carefully, the appropriate Gantt chart is provided on the facing, or following page, while the text describes the gradual unfolding of an event with the current status of the scenario at key touch-points. To help identify IOC processes in train at any time, the following icons are used to inform of the particular process occurring at any time in relation to an event.

info   thought   action   maintenance

Finally, Chapter 9 provides a glimpse of the future IOC, the challenges facing it, and the tools and staff required to operate it.

5

SCENARIO-BASED INFORMATION FLOWS

INTRODUCTION

Chapter 5 is written specially to help bridge the gap between the foundation chapters in Part I of the book, and the scenario-based chapters to follow. Figure 2.1 in Chapter 2 features the key internal relationships among players in the IOC. The range of functional areas included is not exhaustive and certainly varies from airline to airline. But the main purpose is to appreciate the numerous responsibilities and tasks that need to be undertaken in an airline operational environment, whether the roles are segregated as shown in the figure or whether they are contained within the control of a lesser number of individuals. The principal thrust of Chapter 5 is to demonstrate how just a few, selected primary roles might be expanded to explain the deeper levels of communication and involvement that occur not only among the players in the IOC but in terms of the supporting and complementary roles external to the group, such as senior staff, support staff, role specialists and external organisations. What also needs to be kept in mind is that time is of the essence, and as such, all these communications need to happen as quickly as possible. The selection of primary roles is reflected in Figure 5.1.

SCENARIO-BASED INFORMATION FLOWS

Brief

An engineering disruption occurs at the airline's home base. The IOC has been alerted by Maintenance Watch to a technical problem with an aircraft. At this stage, the Engineers attending the aircraft cannot provide an ETS.

IOC Roles

The roles selected in Figure 5.1 present a greatly abridged version of the list in Figure 2.1, showing only a small number of the key functions drawn into this particular problem. Naturally, more roles may become involved in the course of managing a disruption, as will be shown in following chapters, but those disclosed in the current scenario focus on a few key areas. Figures 5.2 to 5.7 present these functional areas as 'contact trails' revealing some of the supporting roles and relationships. It must be taken into account that as all airlines differ markedly, the roles, titles, and the number of levels and hence 'trails' shown vary enormously. Doubtless, each of these figures could be greatly exploded, but they are

Figure 5.1 Internal relationships in the IOC – abridged

shown here to provide at least a basic understanding of some of these relationships.

ENGINEERING CONTACT TRAIL

The disruption is an engineering problem, so Maintenance Watch (in the IOC) are central to the initial advice and then developments throughout the disruption. As mentioned earlier in the book, ensuring the information is valid and received from the appropriate source is vital to the integrity of disruption management. At times, information may be received from well-meaning but ill-informed, non-engineering qualified staff in a port. The information *may* be correct, but reliance on this is fraught with danger until validated by authorised engineering staff. This is one key reason for the location of Maintenance Watch within an IOC. Communications channels between Maintenance Watch and the Engineering Duty Manager (who in turn relies on the expertise of the Engineers attending the aircraft), or the equivalent should a third-party contractor be engaged, can readily assess the nature of a problem and relay this to the Operations Controller. Another position within the Engineering function may be a role with more of an engineering operational support focus, that has contact with airframe or engine type

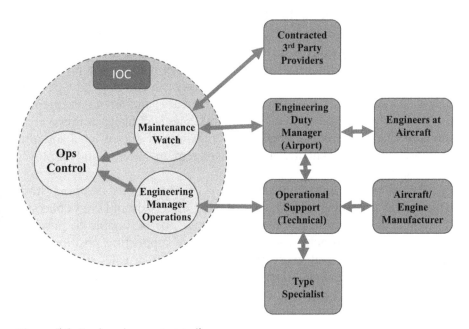

Figure 5.2 Engineering contact trail

specialists or, in some cases, direct with the manufacturers, as presented in Figure 5.2.

The role of Maintenance Watch in the scenario will be to establish the exact nature of the problem, and work with the supporting roles to ascertain what needs to happen to get the aircraft serviceable in the least amount of time. This may mean that parts and other equipment are required to fix or replace components. It is also possible that should the problem be significant, requiring considerably further engineering support, passengers and baggage may have to be removed and the aircraft towed to a hangar. Hence, the communications and actions between the Maintenance Watch personnel and other Engineering roles are critical.

PILOT AND FLIGHT ATTENDANT CREWING CONTACT TRAILS

With an impending or known problem with a flight, the Pilot and Flight Attendant Crew Schedulers on the current day have a sound grasp of any crew-related issues such as where crews originate for the flight, their sign-on and duty times, limitations, assigned duty requirements (i.e., the specific role they are to perform for that flight), flight connections (to or from the flight), overnight bases, and next day commitments, for example. The focus is clearly on managing the crew complements in relation to the immediate flight. They may already be conversing with the operating crews on board the aircraft to establish limitations or request changes to existing rosters. In addition, both Crewing sections are likely to be assessing the potential for further disruption and, even at this early stage, assessing alternative ways to crew both the current flight (should delays be excessive or cancellations be necessary) and any consequential flights which may be affected. To do this, they will likely examine crew member records carefully to ensure any change of duty is legal and also fits work practices, company fatigue-management systems, and employer agreements.

Assisting the Schedulers are 'Day of Operations' support staff, whose roles may include more far-reaching effects should crews become dislodged from patterns, finish 'out of base', or be unable to position for a training assignment, for example. These supporting positions may at times need to consult with specialists in particular roles such as Duty Captains (Pilot Crewing), fleet administration staff, and union officials. Figures 5.3 and 5.4 depict the Crew Scheduler's contact trails for Pilot and Flight Attendant Crewing, respectively.

SCENARIO-BASED INFORMATION FLOWS

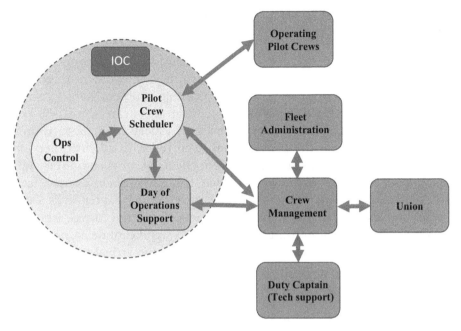

Figure 5.3 Pilot Crewing contact trail

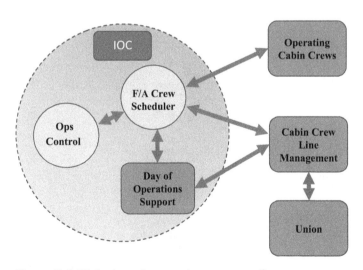

Figure 5.4 Flight Attendant crewing contact trail

SCENARIO-BASED INFORMATION FLOWS

CUSTOMER JOURNEY MANAGEMENT CONTACT TRAIL

The CJM team also become involved in the disruption immediately. Depending upon the timing of the disruption, customers might be in a variety of locations. If the engineering problem has occurred hours before scheduled departure time, customers can be advised not to travel to the airport or given advice of a delayed departure time perhaps. However, if the problem has occurred with all customers on board the aircraft (e.g., during pre-flight checking, or even on start-up) the impact may be more severe. Hence, the CJM processes may need to involve staff at the departure end of travel, looking after VIPs, even removing and offering specified customers alternative travel arrangements rather than undergoing the impact of a significant delay, or worse. Part of the function also assesses the impact at the arrival end, looking at connections beyond the initial destination (both within and external to the airline), accommodation, or immigration issues, for example. Processes such as rebooking of customers onto other flights or assisting them in any other way can be actioned and followed through by customer support staff or officers, or via a third-party contractor. Should matters need to be escalated, there will be a range of people with due responsibility and authority to provide a greater level of support as shown in Figure 5.5.

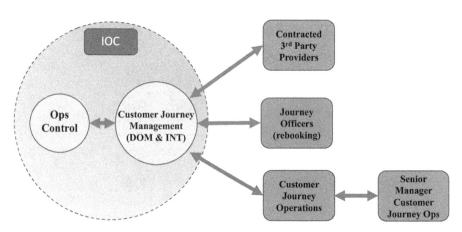

Figure 5.5 Customer Journey Management contact trail

SCENARIO-BASED INFORMATION FLOWS

AIRPORT TRAIL

One of the key functions at each (served) airport is the Port Coordinator or Airport Station Manager/Duty Manager (or some similar name/level). Essentially, this role is an airline role (i.e., it does not belong to the *airport* ownership or operation – rather it is the airline's highest representation at the airport). The Airport Liaison role within the IOC has direct contact with this position at the airports. Therefore communication and passing of information between the two is concise, fast and relevant to the issue at hand. The Port Coordinator/Station Manager ties all the airport functions together, having direct contact with Catering, Fuellers, Engineers, Ramp Officers, terminal staff, airport authorities, ATC, airline partners, competitors, and contracted third-party providers. The position also has oversight of the information systems (flight information display boards) available to staff and the general public. Thus, control of information about delays and cancellations lies not only in the hands of the IOC, but in consultation with the Port Coordinator/Station Manager who has face-to-face contact with the travelling public, and whose workplace may be directly affected by hordes of disrupted (and sometimes angry) travellers, and by congested gates and ramp areas.

The instance of this disruption begins to stretch the airport capability should delays be excessive or flights cancelled. This may be exacerbated at night with subsequent requirements for transport, accommodation and meal vouchers. A delay at the gate in a busy terminal may have consequential effects for arriving traffic due to limited parking places. In some airports, where dedicated gates suit certain aircraft types, further complexities arise. Figure 5.6 depicts the Airport contact trail.

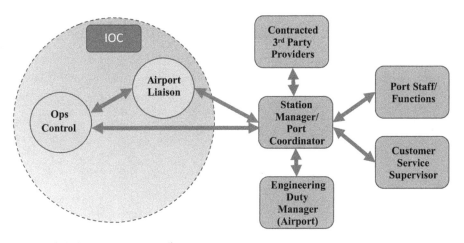

Figure 5.6 Airport contact trail

SCENARIO-BASED INFORMATION FLOWS

DISPATCH/SLOT CONTROL CONTACT TRAIL

Decisions emanating from Operations Control will have ramifications for the Dispatch function (and through that function, Flight Planning/Navigation/Load Control services). Should the engineering problem result in delayed or cancelled services, change of aircraft or flight number, for example, notification to ATC is necessary. Where either or both departure and arrival airports are slot constrained, the Slot Controller (or equivalent) in the IOC may also need to negotiate alternative arrangements with the Air Service Provider, as shown in Figure 5.7.

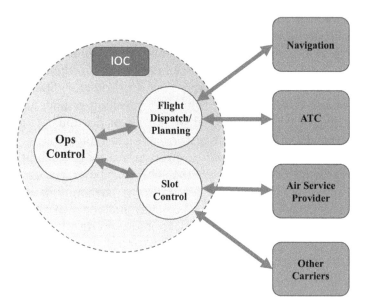

Figure 5.7 Dispatch/Slot Control contact trail

Bearing in mind the background information described in Part I of the book, and the nature of communications in and beyond the IOC described in this chapter, the following chapters draw on this in a fully practical sense, as three scenarios are examined in some detail. At this stage, there should be sufficient knowledge gained to follow and understand the impact of airline disruptions on the travelling public and the vast resources, expertise and capabilities the airline employs to minimise outcomes.

WEATHER SCENARIO: *SNOW AT JFK AIRPORT*

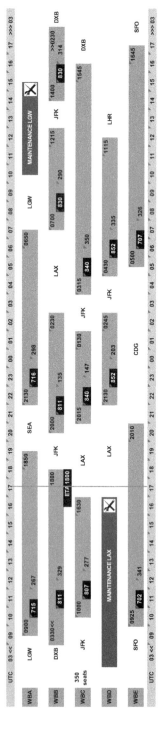

Figure 6.1 JFK weather – status @ 1700

- All times in the scenario relate to UTC time.
- A timeline indicates the current time in the scenario.
- Prior to the timeline, all flights are operating on schedule
- Flight numbers are shown on dark background
- Actual booked loadings are shown to the right of the flight numbers
- Flights exceeding timescale are shown with << or >>
- For this scenario, LHR and LGW are UTC time, CDG is UTC + 1 hr, DXB is UTC + 4 hrs, JFK, CLE are UTC – 5 hrs, ORD is UTC – 6 hrs, SEA, SFO and LAX are UTC – 8 hrs.
- The utilisation is not intended to simulate any existing airlines. It is only a representation.

6
WEATHER SCENARIO:
SNOW AT JFK AIRPORT

BRIEF

The airline has an international operation using five twin-engine, wide-body, long-range aircraft (registrations/tails designated WBA-WBE). The capacity of the aircraft is 350 seats. Minimum turnaround time between passenger flights is 90 minutes. Refer to Figure 6.1 opposite.

SCENARIO DESCRIPTION

The time is 1700 UTC. A snowstorm is affecting New York's JFK airport in the US and conditions have been marginal since early morning. However, the airport is not closed and traffic is still operating, although some national and regional carriers have suspended a number of services into and out of JFK. Due to the high volumes of traffic in the area and the requirement for instrument approaches, several aircraft have been placed in holding patterns around JFK. WBB operating Flight 811 DXB-JFK is scheduled to arrive JFK at 1800. Flight 811 was dispatched from DXB with sufficient fuel for three (3) hours' holding using CLE (Cleveland – 370 NM west of JFK) as the alternate for JFK. ATC have just advised the aircraft that they can now expect three (3) hours' holding at JFK and at 1740, the aircraft entered a holding pattern 80 NM east.

WEATHER SCENARIO: *SNOW AT JFK AIRPORT*

IOC INTERACTION

 The JFK Station Manager has advised the IOC that 811 has been given holding for up to three hours to the east of JFK. No further information has been forwarded.

The IOC now needs to establish a number of things.

a) What is the reason for the unexpected, extended holding time? (Weather holding was expected (and was planned for, in the initial flight plan) but the concern is for the reason underlying the additional holding.)
b) What are conditions expected to be like both in the air and on the ground for this later arrival? (Are conditions generally improving or worsening and is that revised time accurate or just a possibility?)
c) What is the aircraft's maximum holding time now at JFK? (Given the additional holding time, the expectation would be that the holding would exceed the aircraft's capability, immediately raising the concern of a diversion.)
d) What alternates are valid if the aircraft holds for the three hours? (Selecting a different alternate may enable the aircraft to continue holding over JFK for longer, always with the possibility that the holding may be reduced and the aircraft given an approach.)
e) Are other aircraft getting approaches into JFK? (This may be a good predictor of a likely landing provided that conditions are not deteriorating.)
f) Crew hours may be a concern also, and pre-emptive questioning of Crewing will also determine the nearest relief crew should a diversion occur.
g) Would it be better for the aircraft to divert *now* with the hope of returning to JFK, rather than wait until the three hours' holding time expires, then divert and subsequently run out of crew hours?
h) Should the 811 JFK-LAX crew be held at the hotel (to delay signing on until it is known that the aircraft will definitely land?

Refer to Figure 6.2 opposite.

WEATHER SCENARIO: *SNOW AT JFK AIRPORT*

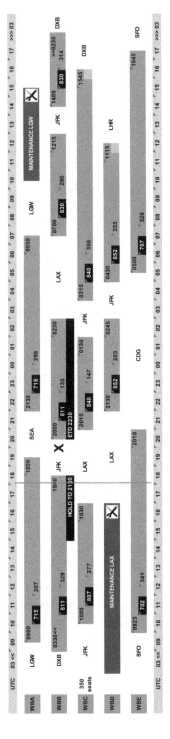

Figure 6.2 JFK weather – status @ 1740

WEATHER SCENARIO: *SNOW AT JFK AIRPORT*

 Once the answers to these questions are received and assessed, consideration for any action begins. At this stage, though, there is little action the IOC can take, other than starting to look at options should the aircraft have to divert. A key task of the IOC is communicating with its stakeholders, so an update of the situation will be provided for the IOC functional areas (e.g., Crewing, CJM, Media). What will be of immediate concern to the CJM staff is the on-carriage – the number of connections that now may be at risk. Conversations and updates with the port of JFK and, if possible, direct with the aircraft Captain using SATCOM will help to complete the picture.

At this stage, a delay to 811 JFK-LAX is expected (as depicted in Figure 6.2), but the IOC will be reluctant to set a delay of three hours, based on the advised holding time given to WBB by ATC. Often, circumstances such as weather and air traffic conditions can change, with the result that the holding time can be reduced significantly, or alternatively, extended further. The IOC will therefore be conservative with setting a delay time as customers are advised, and staffing and resources matched with the later schedule. The IOC though, will begin to look at what-if scenarios. If WBB holds for, say, 1–2 hours, and then lands, then 811 simply operates late to LAX with no further consequence to the network. But if the aircraft were to divert, the recovery of customers and aircraft becomes more complex. At this stage, updated information will inform the next process.

UPDATE @ 1915 UTC

 The weather at JFK has not improved, and currently several aircraft are still holding, although some domestic carriers have diverted. WBB 811 has been holding for about 90 minutes to the east of New York at cruising altitude (to minimise fuel burn). The Cleveland Department of Port Control (DPC; which manages and operates CLE airport) now advises that although the weather at CLE is still conducive to operations, the airport has become logjammed. This is due to severe congestion on the ground caused by several earlier diversions, and there is no longer gate availability. For this reason, the DPC have advised that CLE is now unsuitable as an alternate for JFK. This advice is received by the IOC from the JFK Station Manager, who gathers information from, and is updated by, the Local Port Authority.

The crew of 811 are advised accordingly. As a result, WBB have notified that they are diverting immediately to ORD (643 NM west of JFK), with an ETA of 2120. Refer to Figure 6.3 opposite. The circled

WEATHER SCENARIO: *SNOW AT JFK AIRPORT*

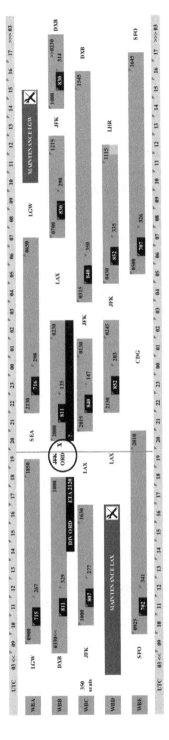

Figure 6.3 JFK weather – status @ 1915

WEATHER SCENARIO: *SNOW AT JFK AIRPORT*

alert (just as a highlight in this example) indicates the diversion and the fact that due to this, there is now no aircraft at JFK to operate 811 JFK-LAX, with subsequent impact on the rest of the flying pattern for WBB.

 The IOC now has several issues to consider. The first ones involve the diverted aircraft.

a) Once the aircraft arrives at ORD, would it be worth fuelling up and trying to get back into JFK? The chances are that a similar ATC holding time (or worse, due to the build-up of traffic) would be applied, if indeed ATC provided a slot at all. Even if this were possible, would the crew have sufficient hours to fly this additional leg?

b) Of the total customer load on the aircraft, the IOC also needs to determine how many customers are travelling DXB-JFK and how many are travelling DXB-LAX. (If the airline has carriage rights within the USA, another consideration would be for any customers booked JFK-LAX.) *In the current scenario 194 customers are bound for JFK with 135 for LAX. There is none booked JFK-LAX.*

c) If the aircraft stays in ORD, is there accommodation for the 329 customers? Even if accommodation were readily available, how and when will these customers subsequently be moved from ORD back to JFK? The Station Manager together with the CJM team, would address such a situation once a decision is made regarding recovery options.

d) With the crew likely to be out of hours at ORD and unable to take the aircraft back to JFK, the aircraft is also unable to continue as 811 to LAX (as the crew for the JFK-LAX flight are in JFK). Crewing will be aware of the diversion to ORD and the unlikelihood of the aircraft returning to JFK immediately, so that (1) they know their inbound crew will now finish in ORD, out of hours and out of position for their next duty commitments, and (2) they can stop the new 811 JFK-LAX crew from signing on at least until a recovery plan is determined.

e) The diversion causes three further problems: First is that the DXB-JFK and DXB-LAX customers currently will not get to their destinations as planned. Second, is that 329 customers are stuck in ORD who should not be there, and third, with the aircraft terminating at ORD, there is no aircraft in LAX to operate 830 LAX-JFK at 0700.

f) The IOC needs to ascertain if there is any *aircraft*, and from both Crewing functions if there are any *crews* in the vicinity or who could be positioned, to assist recovery. (If the airline had scheduled flights into nearby ports, there may well be operations that could assist. In the current scenario though, the utilisation depicted is complete.

g) This level of thinking requires a detailed scan of the Gantt chart (Figure 6.3).

UPDATE @ 1930 UTC

Viewing the Gantt chart (Figure 6.3) reveals related issues.

a) With the time now at about 1930, Flight 840 LAX-JFK (WBC) is about to depart (at 2015). With 811 having diverted, the question as to whether 840 should depart on time, be delayed, or even operate at all, needs to be raised.

b) 840 would need to carry several hours holding fuel at JFK, with the expectation of being able to land. The flight duration is 5 hours 15 min, so the expected weather at 0130 will determine the likelihood of landing at that time. Given the current conditions and forecast, one or more alternates will be planned, and operating the flight certainly ensures an aircraft for Flight 840 to continue to DXB (provided it can first land at JFK).

c) Further examination of the chart reveals another Flight LAX-JFK just behind 840 scheduled to depart LAX at 2130. This is 852 (WBD).

d) Are these two flights combinable (i.e., do the total customer loads fit in one aircraft?), as one thought may be to consider sending only one aircraft to JFK and using the other to rescue WBB in ORD?

e) The combined customer load is 350 (147 on FLT840 + 203 on FLT852), all of whom fit onto this aircraft type. Therefore, an option would then be to cancel one of these flights. The preference is 840 LAX-JFK rather than 852 LAX-JFK, because the 840 customers are already at the gate (45 minutes before departure), while the 852 customers will still be checking in at the terminal, and would not be processed in time for the earlier of the two flights. There's also the preferred opportunity of maintaining 852 on schedule.

f) To combine the flights would mean stopping the departure process of 840 right away until a full plan is conceived. This can take quite a while with many IOC functions involved, as well as the airport staff in the terminal and the ramp staff currently preparing the aircraft. At 1930, 840 would be about to board its customers, will still be in the process of being loaded with freight, baggage and catering, and may also be onloading fuel.

WEATHER SCENARIO: *SNOW AT JFK AIRPORT*

g) Another consideration is the weight of the aircraft. For example, combining the loads, together with the high fuel figure needed for LAX-JFK (that includes holding time and alternate fuel in case of diversion) may place the aircraft overweight, especially for landing, so liaison with Load Control/Dispatch (subject to the airline) would establish this and any action that may be necessary. The carriage of the fuel amount is essential to meet operating conditions, so the only flexibility available will be varying the payload. Customers and baggage will be prioritised over freight in these circumstances and consideration also has to be given to the actual conditions on the ramp in JFK; it would be prudent to limit any ground-handling processes to minimise risk to both people and equipment. The response from Load Control/Dispatch as to exactly how heavy the aircraft will be, and which limitations will be potentially exceeded, may further influence the IOC decision. Of course, the 840 Operating Captain is already either on board or close to the aircraft, and therefore able to be consulted with regard to final weights and any limitations.

h) Finally, the crews needed to operate a rescue plan will result in some crews being taken off their planned patterns which may affect their return to their base or create other changes down-line. This lies in the domain of the Crewing function to resolve, but providing the crews can help the recovery process at the time, this may still prove to be part of the optimum solution.

i) This is only part of the solution, as working out exactly what to do with the aircraft in ORD in terms of ways to 'match up' the patterns again needs to be considered. If WBD 852 operates on schedule, that aircraft simply continues to LHR. However, with no aircraft in JFK to operate 840 JFK-DXB, further change is needed.

j) The scan of the chart will quickly identify any other aircraft that may be operating in/across the country (such as WBA and WBE). In this case, compromising their operations would be quickly dismissed as there would be no gain, and in reality, further disruption. Nevertheless, experienced Controllers are well aware of their total network operations – this is the value of the familiarisation stages following the briefing at the commencement of shift and this approach is what sets the expert Controllers apart from others.

UPDATE @ 1945 UTC

Taking the various inputs into consideration, weighing up the optimum customer-recovery process, and ensuring the best outcome in terms of maintaining schedule integrity, the IOC is now in a position to put a plan into action to resolve the problem and recover operations (based on given information and no further change).

This plan is likely to consist of the following (as depicted by Figure 6.4 overleaf):

a) Cancel 840 LAX-JFK, with all 147 customers accommodated on 852 LAX-JFK (these customers are delayed 75 minutes). This action needs a high priority to ensure WBC is unloaded and the combined load placed onto WBD as efficiently as possible. Ideally 852 is not delayed itself.

b) Cancel 811 JFK-LAX. (Of course, there is now no aircraft at JFK to operate this service and there are no originating customers for this flight.)

c) With 840 LAX-JFK cancelled, WBC can be used to operate a ferry or positioning flight as 9901 LAX-ORD (airlines have a bank of spare numbers for this purpose), using the 840 full crew (tech crew and Flight Attendants) with a departure time probably by 2100). This aircraft then operates the diverted Flight 811 (as the continuation of this flight) on an ORD-JFK sector (clearly – subject to the weather at JFK by the time this aircraft arrives), thereby getting all the DXB-JFK customers to their destination. This also provides an aircraft to operate 840 JFK-DXB, albeit with a delay of about 135 minutes (as depicted in Figure 6.4).

d) For the 135 DXB-LAX customers who are still in ORD, the options would amount to a decision taken between the CJM team and the handling agent at ORD (as this is not a standard airline port). Either they could be dispersed onto other domestic services, bearing in mind that for some of these customers, LAX may not be their final destination, so specific travel recovery will be enacted for them. Alternatively, subject to the next point, they may be able to travel on 9902 ORD-LAX provided that Flight Attendants can crew this flight.

e) An attempt would be made to get the first available crew to dead-head (position) to ORD on a commercial flight in order to operate 9902 ORD-LAX. This may be the original 811 JFK-LAX crew, provided a suitable flight was operating and could depart JFK in the current weather. Alternatively, there may be a crew in LAX who could dead-head

WEATHER SCENARIO: *SNOW AT JFK AIRPORT*

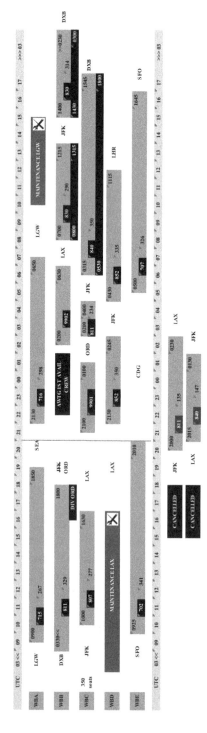

Figure 6.4 JFK weather – solution

on 9901 LAX-ORD (to operate 9902 ORD-LAX). The downside of this is that should a crew be available in LAX, a call-out is likely to take several hours, thereby delaying 9901 considerably (and as a consequence, 811 ORD-JFK, 840 JFK-DXB and 9902 ORD-LAX). At worst, the technical crew that brought the diverted aircraft into ORD could be used after crew rest (possibly 12 hours subject to duty and rest provisions). This would achieve 9902 ORD-LAX but without customers. If Flight Attendants are included in the crew, then 9902 can carry the 135 DXB-LAX customers.

f) In summary, two flights (840 LAX-JFK, 811 JFK-LAX) are being cancelled and two flights are being added (9901 LAX-ORD, 9902 ORD-LAX), achieving continuation of journey for the 811 customers (ORD-JFK) and ensuring aircraft are positioned appropriately. Some delays have been inevitable but are unavoidable in such a situation.

g) The CJM team (together with local management) will be responsible for accommodating customers on available services.

FINAL COMMENT

Figure 6.4 indicates how the resolved situation may look on the Gantt chart. The solution in this scenario achieves optimum customer satisfaction given the circumstances, recovers the aircraft and crew patterns fairly and efficiently, and minimises the effects on this part of the network. The solution, of course, relied on weather conditions enabling subsequent operations to continue through JFK.

WEATHER SCENARIO: *THUNDERSTORMS AT SYD*

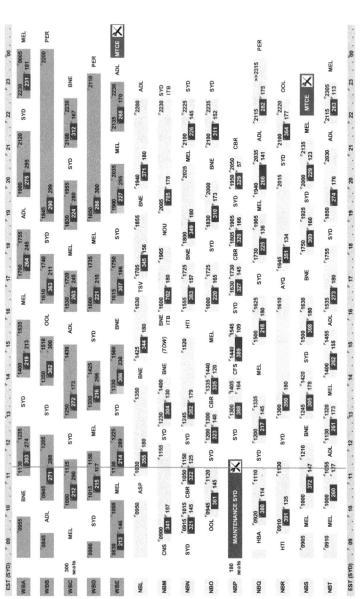

Figure 7.1 SYD weather – status @ 1115

- All times in the scenario relate to EST (SYD) time.
- The chart is depicted in Eastern Standard time (SYD time). Blocks/PUKs are *positioned* according to this time, but *displayed* according to *local* port arrival and departure times (e.g., *local* time in ADL or NOU).
- A timeline indicates the current time in the scenario.
- Prior to the timeline, all flights are operating on schedule.
- Flight numbers are shown on dark background.
- Actual booked loadings are shown to the right of the flight numbers.
- Flights exceeding timescale are shown with << or >>
- For this scenario, NOU is EST + 1 hr, CNS, TSV, HTI, BNE, OOL, SYD, CBR, MEL and HBA are EST – ½ hr, PER is EST – 2 hrs.
- Curfews (2300–0600) exist at ADL, OOL and SYD.

158

7

WEATHER SCENARIO: *THUNDERSTORMS AT SYD AIRPORT*

BRIEF

The airline is a domestic carrier in Australia. The fleet consists of five twin-engine, wide-body aircraft (registrations/tails designated WBA-WBE), and nine twin-engine narrow-body (single-aisle) aircraft (registrations designated NBL-NBT). The capacity of the wide-body aircraft is 300 seats and the narrow-body aircraft 180 seats. Minimum turnaround time between passenger flights for wide-body aircraft is 60 minutes and for narrow-body aircraft is 35 minutes.

Refer to Figure 7.1 opposite.

WEATHER SCENARIO: *THUNDERSTORMS AT SYD*

Scenario Description

The time is 1115 EST (SYD) Time. Several lines of severe thunderstorms are approaching SYD. The IOC's Meteorological section has been aware of imminent thunderstorms during the morning and forewarned of the most likely impact time. Previously issued terminal area forecasts (TAFs) indicate that from 1130–1230, SYD can expect sustained winds from the west in excess of 40 knots as a frontal system moves through. In addition, low cloud, heavy rain, lightning on and around the airport and severe turbulence below 5000 ft can be expected. The current METAR indicates variable winds favouring the north from 15–20 knots. Accordingly, the two parallel runways, 34L and 34R are currently in use. Aircraft en route to SYD and due to arrive from 1030 onwards, have been required to carry sufficient fuel to be able to divert to an alternate airport (alternate fuel).

IOC Interaction

(i) The airline's SYD Port Coordinator has advised that thunderstorms are expected in the immediate SYD area in the next 15 minutes. She has established that NBQ 380 HBA-SYD and WBC 212 MEL-SYD are currently holding south of SYD, and NBO 361 OOL-SYD is holding to the north, but no further information is available yet. Further, she advised that ATC are expecting the winds to change, and aircraft are likely to be held further while the front passes through. Currently, aircraft are departing SYD without delay, and aircraft have been landing on both the parallel runways.

💡 The immediate concern in the IOC is for flights about to arrive into SYD, and then for others that are already en route, but not yet in the vicinity. A full scan of the utilisation reveals the considerable number of aircraft close to SYD (refer to Figure 7.1). The scan not only looks at the imminent arrivals but extends across each pattern to assess the potential consequential impact should they be disrupted. The stand-out information will include the amounts of ground time (where delays may get absorbed), patterns leading to curfews (e.g., WBA (SYD), WBE (ADL), NBM (SYD), NBN (SYD), NBO (SYD) and NBR (OOL)), and any irregular flights (e.g., charters, ferry flights or international operations), as these may require specific attention (e.g., NBM operating BNE-NOU-SYD).

Information needs to be established about each of the inbound aircraft, from two points of view. The first is to establish a likely sequence of approaches from ATC, which will assist the IOC in determining which aircraft are likely to land first, such that departures can be prioritised. The second concerns the identification of longer haul inbound aircraft that may not be able to hold for very long. The questions are likely to include the following:

a) Where is each aircraft (i.e., on descent, approach or already in a holding pattern)?
b) What fuel is each carrying?
c) How long can each hold?
d) What alternate has each nominated?

The received information may reveal the status of many of the aircraft, but often the information comes through spasmodically, or not at all (everyone is busy at this time – especially ATC), in which case it must be sought from the appropriate area. In this scenario, the following information (in order of scheduled arrival time) has now been ascertained by the Port Coordinator and advised to the IOC at 1120:

a) NBQ 380 HBA-SYD (due at 1110) has been given 20 mins holding south of the field. NBQ has 20 mins of holding fuel before having to divert using CBR as its alternate.
b) NBO 361 OOL-SYD (due at 1120) has been given 15 mins holding north of the field, and has 30 mins of holding fuel before having to divert using OOL as its alternate.
c) WBC 212 MEL-SYD (due at 1125) has been given 15 mins holding south of the field, and has 40 mins of holding fuel before having to divert using MEL as its alternate.
d) NBR 391 HTI-SYD (due at 1130) has been given 30 mins holding north of the field, and has 45 mins of holding fuel before having to divert using OOL as its alternate.
e) NBN 322 CBR-SYD (due at 1150) has been given 35 mins holding south-west of the field, and has 60 mins of holding fuel before having to divert using CBR as its alternate.
f) NBM 341 CNS-SYD (due at 1155) has been given 40 mins holding north of the field, and has 35 mins of holding fuel before having to divert using OOL as its alternate.
g) WBB 271 ADL-SYD (due at 1205) has been given 30 mins holding west of the field, and has 60 mins of holding fuel before having to divert using BNE as its alternate.

WEATHER SCENARIO: *THUNDERSTORMS AT SYD*

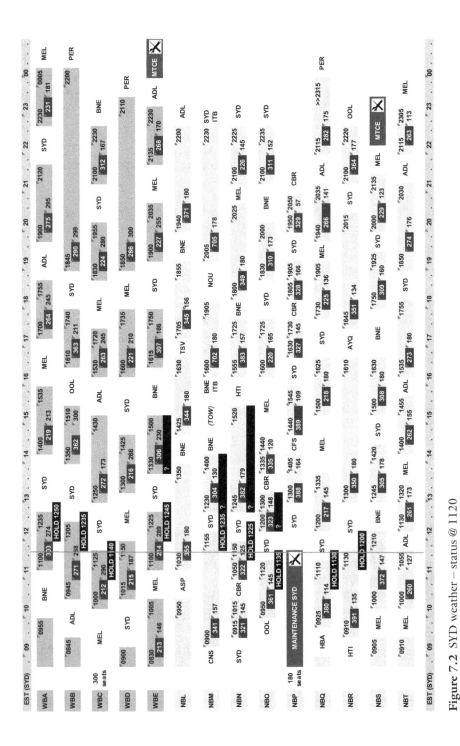

Figure 7.2 SYD weather – status @ 1120

h) WBE 214 MEL-SYD (due at 1225) has been told by ATC to expect 20 mins holding west of the field. WBE has just got airborne at MEL and has 50 mins of holding fuel before having to divert using MEL as its alternate.

i) WBA 303 BNE-SYD (due at 1235) has been told by ATC to expect 15 mins holding. WBA has just got airborne at BNE and has 65 mins of holding fuel before having to divert using BNE as its alternate.

With this information the IOC can start to address potential delays likely to affect the network.

Figure 7.2 opposite reflects the holding times above.

Of immediate concern are the first aircraft due into SYD, with NBQ (ETA 1130), NBO (ETA 1135) and WBC (ETA 1140), being given short holding times. However, the information received about NBM's status is of immediate concern, as the aircraft has been given 40 minutes holding which is in excess of its 35 minutes reserve fuel. Thus, the IOC will need to clarify this information, and if correct, need to establish the intention of the crew. This would be achieved via the Port Coordinator, direct with ATC, or direct with the crew by radio (contacting the crew when their workload is high may be difficult, so sometimes a relay through ATC is necessary). A further consideration is whether the aircraft is able to hold for longer using a different alternate. In other words, can the aircraft use a closer diversion port which would increase its holding time? Also of concern are the next aircraft commitments for those that have been given holding. In particular, WBE 306 SYD-BNE, NBM 304 SYD-BNE, NBN 382 SYD-HTI and NBO 323 SYD-CBR will potentially be delayed as the utilisation currently stands (i.e., no aircraft swaps made).

UPDATE @ 1122 EST

SYD Port Coordinator advises the following update.

a) NBM has diverted to OOL due to holding requirements (ETA OOL is 1205).

b) NBQ, NBO and WBC in sequence have all been given an approach (using RWY34L).

c) NBQ crew has advised that they have enough fuel for one approach and, if not successful, will divert to CBR.

WEATHER SCENARIO: *THUNDERSTORMS AT SYD*

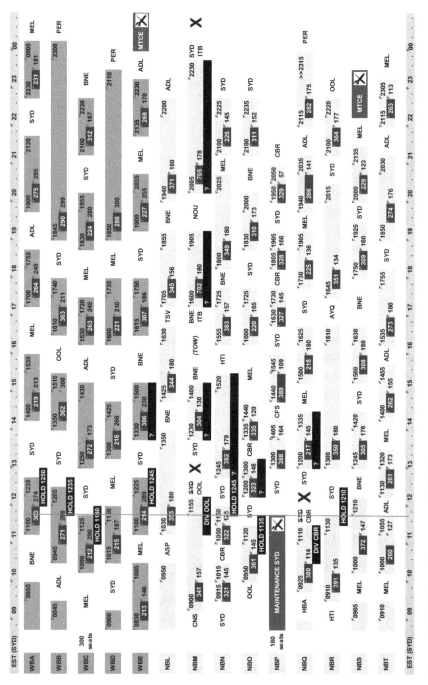

Figure 7.3 SYD weather – status @ 1125

WEATHER SCENARIO: *THUNDERSTORMS AT SYD*

d) The weather conditions on the ground still favour RWYs 34L/R and the airport is open for all operations, although heavy rain has commenced, and wind speed increased.

The diversion of NBM was not surprising, given the information received about its fuel reserves and the ATC holding requirements. The fundamental thought is the aircraft's next commitment, while Crewing consider the crew commitments and the CJM team consider tranships beyond SYD. The CJM team will also start to examine ways to get the CNS-SYD customers to SYD should the IOC need to send the aircraft elsewhere. The aircraft is currently committed for 304 SYD-BNE (indicated by an 'x' on Figure 7.3), followed by the international operation 702/705 BNE-NOU-SYD with a subsequent curfew limitation in SYD.

UPDATE @ 1125 EST

SYD Port Coordinator relays the next update.

a) NBQ has just had a missed approach due to wind shear on final, and has diverted to CBR (ETA CBR is 1220).
b) NBO is about to have an approach.
c) Not sure of the whereabouts of WBC; trying to find out from ATC.
d) NBR has been given additional 10 minutes holding (hold until 1210).
e) NBN has been given additional 20 minutes holding (hold until 1245).

In the IOC, the CJM team advise that NBN 322 CBR-SYD has a 45-member joint Australian and Noumea Government delegation of senior ministers and their respective departmental staff travelling to Noumea on 322 CBR-SYD/304 SYD-BNE/702 BNE-NOU. With this latest information – notably the diversions and the government travel, the IOC needs to consider the immediate impact, in particular the likelihood of NBN landing in SYD.

The Gantt chart is likely to be updated as shown in Figure 7.3 opposite.

The diversion of NBQ to CBR results in another shortage of aircraft in SYD, this time to operate 217 SYD-MEL (indicated by an 'x' on Figure 7.3). Now with the loss of two aircraft in the SYD area, the IOC would start to consider cancellations in order to re-balance the flights. An orderly consideration of issues may appear as follows:

WEATHER SCENARIO: *THUNDERSTORMS AT SYD*

a) With NBQ diverting to CBR, either this aircraft could just refuel and operate back to SYD or a SYD-CBR flight could be cancelled. The problem with getting NBQ back to SYD is exacerbated by the deteriorating weather conditions at SYD and the accumulation of holding as a result, so in all probability this would take several hours. Thus, the thought may be for cancelling 323 SYD-CBR (currently NBO), and by swapping patterns around, using NBQ to operate 335 CBR-MEL as this would be a ready solution and would also help to preserve the schedule for the remainder of that current flying pattern. If NBQ did not refuel and operate back to SYD, a search of the Reservations system would be conducted to establish any seats CBR-SYD available to uplift the HBA-SYD customers, preferably on the next CBR-SYD flight (or if necessary, on a competitor's), and similarly, ways to uplift the 323 customers SYD-CBR. The SYD-CBR customers can in fact all be accommodated on 327 departing at 1630 (35 seats) and 329 departing at 1950 (123 seats). However, only 14 seats are available CBR-SYD (on 328 departing CBR at 1805). As CBR-SYD is about four hours road time, a feasible customer recovery may include the use of buses CBR-SYD for many of the diverted 380 HBA-SYD customers.

b) With NBM diverting to OOL, there is a shortage of aircraft in SYD for 304 SYD-BNE and scanning across the utilisation, this can be seen as a critical flight, as within its ground time in BNE (2 hours), the aircraft needs to be unloaded, towed from the domestic to the international terminal, and then readied for an international operation (702 BNE-NOU), requiring additional preparation than for a domestic service. Delaying this service also has curfew implications in SYD.

c) The main consideration for NBM is whether to ferry this aircraft OOL-BNE such that it could operate 702/705 BNE-NOU-SYD on schedule, or whether it should refuel and operate immediately to SYD, which guarantees that the CNS-SYD customers get to SYD without further disruption, and also covers the growing shortfall of aircraft in the SYD area. Further, it may serve as insurance in case other aircraft divert from SYD. The occasion of thunderstorms often is limited in time and impact, and if NBM were to depart OOL at 1230, the aircraft would not be in the SYD area until 1400, well after the storms have passed. As this sector is considerably shorter than CNS-SYD, a greater fuel load can be uplifted with a longer holding time (if necessary).

d) The status of NBN now also comes into play, as (i) it has been given further holding such that it is now very close to the latest diversion

WEATHER SCENARIO: *THUNDERSTORMS AT SYD*

time for CBR and (ii) it has the governmental delegation on board for Noumea. A number of thought processes in the IOC could consider the range of options as follows.

i. The first may be to request the NBN 322 crew to calculate whether they can use BNE as their alternate instead of CBR, and if so (bearing in mind the additional distance to BNE compared with CBR), what would then be their latest divert time? Diverting NBN to BNE has merit – it would both guarantee an aircraft for 702 BNE-NOU on schedule and importantly, facilitate connection for the government delegation. Weighing against that, though, is the impact for the other CBR-SYD customers on the flight as they would travel via BNE and then need to be accommodated on the next available BNE-SYD flight (this would be 307 WBE which has 114 vacant seats) and would arrive in SYD at 1750.

ii. The second option if NBN cannot use BNE as the alternate, is for the aircraft to divert to CBR, refuel, then operate back to SYD, weather permitting. However, this option revisits the situation described in (c) above, requiring NBM to ferry OOL-BNE to operate 702/705 BNE-NOU-SYD, with the CNS-SYD customers either misplaced in OOL or taken to BNE for next available uplift to SYD.

iii. The third option if NBN were to divert to CBR, would be to cancel 322 CBR-SYD and send the aircraft direct CBR-BNE. NBN is holding south of SYD, so if it diverted immediately, it would arrive CBR at about 1215, could re-depart at about 1245 and arrive BNE at 1425. This may cause a small delay on 702 BNE-NOU, but would provide an aircraft and facilitate the connection for the government delegation as described above. The 322 CBR-SYD customers would then be accommodated as described in point (a) above.

UPDATE @ 1128 EST

SYD Port Coordinator advises the following update.

a) The crew of NBN have replied to the request. They confirm that they can nominate BNE as the alternate but *must divert within 2 minutes.*
b) NBO has just had a missed approach due to strong cross-winds. NBO has enough fuel for one further approach, before diverting to OOL.
c) WBC is now holding again south of the field. An approach is not expected within 30 minutes.

WEATHER SCENARIO: *THUNDERSTORMS AT SYD*

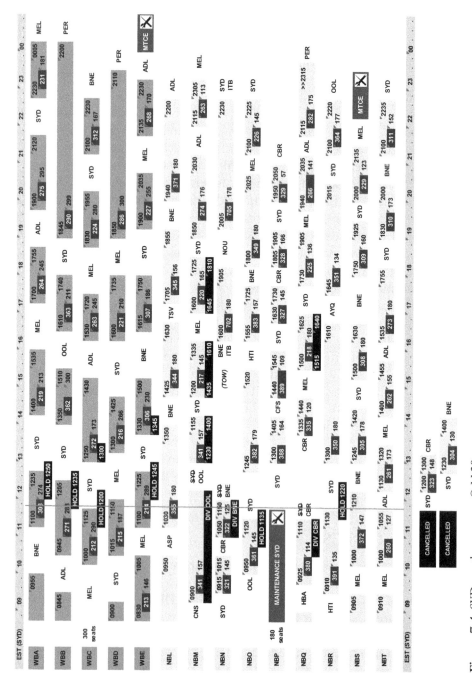

Figure 7.4 SYD weather – status @ 1130

WEATHER SCENARIO: *THUNDERSTORMS AT SYD*

The decision regarding NBN lies within the IOC. The advantages of diverting the aircraft to BNE override the convenience of returning to CBR. With NBO now missing its approach, the shortage of aircraft in SYD is again threatened. Therefore, considerations need be given to remove some more flying so as to relieve the commitments whereby preference is likely to be given to routes that have alternative uplift for customers. As SYD-CFS-SYD only operates once in the day, SYD-HTI-BNE and SYD-AYQ-SYD are both longer haul services and should be commercially protected, the SYD-MEL-SYD or SYD-BNE-SYD routes which have higher frequencies provide part of the solution. Accordingly, removing flights from (at least) one of these will free-up the utilisation. Flight 304 SYD-BNE currently does not have an aircraft to operate the service (since NBM diverted to OOL), and the involvement of NBN in the BNE services as well, helps to form a picture whereby 304 becomes a prime candidate for cancellation.

The IOC immediately invokes a series of actions. Delaying decisions at this point will render some options unavailable, as the decision-making window can be extremely small in domestic disruptions. Numerous aircraft changes (all within type) are now actioned (refer to Figure 7.4 opposite) to protect longer haul sectors and curfews, while minimising delays overall. For disrupted customers, the CJM team take appropriate action to contact them, rebook them onto other services, and arrange ground transport as necessary.

a) Instruct (via the Port Coordinator/ATC) NBN 322 CBR-SYD to divert to BNE immediately. The aircraft then operates 702 BNE-NOU, 705 NOU-SYD on schedule.
b) Cancel 323 SYD-CBR (see cancelled flights at the foot of Figure 7.4).
c) Cancel 304 SYD-BNE (see cancelled flights at the foot of Figure 7.4).
d) NBM to refuel in OOL and continue 341 OOL-SYD. The consideration then is to decide how to give preference for SYD departures. As explained above, 388/389 SYD-CFS-SYD and 382/383 SYD-HTI-BNE flights are not likely to be affected. Similarly, commercial preference would be given for 350/351 SYD-AYQ-SYD to operate on schedule. Thus, the decision to delay 217 SYD-MEL/218 MEL-SYD would be made. However, as NBQ will be in MEL and can operate 218 earlier than NBM, NBM operates 220 MEL-SYD instead, then 274 SYD-ADL and 263 ADL-MEL. Other changes are then made to provide most flights on schedule while protecting all curfews.
e) NBO (based upon the aircraft getting into SYD and not diverting) operates 382 SYD-HTI, 383 HTI-BNE, 349 BNE-MEL and 226 MEL-SYD.

WEATHER SCENARIO: *THUNDERSTORMS AT SYD*

f) After 335 CBR-MEL, NBQ operates 218 MEL-SYD with only a small delay, then 225 SYD-MEL, 266 MEL-ADL and 282 ADL-PER on schedule.

g) After 273 ADL-SYD, NBT operates 310/311 SYD-BNE-SYD.

h) Note that for NBQ to operate 335 CBR-MEL, liaison between the Ops Controller and both Crewing sections (Pilot and Flight Attendant) will determine what crews are available in CBR. One (perhaps obvious) solution would be to use the 380 HBA-SYD crews who brought the aircraft into CBR, but there may be crewing limitations that prevent this. There may also be crews originating in CBR who can operate 335. Had an aircraft other than NBQ been changed to overnight PER (where there are minimal maintenance facilities), liaison would have been required with Maintenance Watch to ensure the aircraft has sufficient maintenance release hours (i.e., does not need a check service overnight) and does not have other critical maintenance work pending. However, despite the changes within the utilisation, very little overnight base changing has been actioned in this scenario.

The changes reflecting these actions are shown in Figure 7.4.

UPDATE @ 1132 EST

(i) SYD Port Coordinator advises the following update.

a) The front is passing through. Winds have changed to Westerly, blowing from 240–280 degrees, at 20–30 knots, gusting to 45 knots.

b) Accordingly, the duty runway has now been changed to RWY25. (The loss of the dual north–south runways and the reduction to a single runway will add to congestion and holding times, as movement rates are considerably reduced).

c) With the arrival of the storm on the airport, lightning is now within 5 NM. As a consequence, all staff have been ordered off the tarmac. Aircraft can still land and take off but, in these circumstances, may have to hold off their bay until the 5 NM warning has been retracted.

d) NBO is holding to the east of the airport and, as advised earlier, has sufficient fuel for one more approach, but can only hold until 1150 anyway before diverting to OOL.

e) WBC has been given another 20 minutes holding (south of the airport).

WEATHER SCENARIO: *THUNDERSTORMS AT SYD*

Maintenance Watch advise that the Engineers at the hangar cannot tow NBP from the hangar to the terminal due to the lightning at the airport. The aircraft will not be on-line until 1245.

UPDATE @ 1145 EST

SYD Port Coordinator advises the following update.

a) The lightning activity has passed and normal operations resumed.
b) From ATC, NBO will be the first aircraft on approach.
c) WBC (by radio) advises it must have an approach by 1150 or divert to MEL.

With other changes under way and a reasonable solution to cover the disruptions so far, attention turns to both NBO and WBC. If NBO were to divert, the next likely 'casualty' will be 388/389 SYD-CFS-SYD, with commercial preference to protect the longer haul HTI and AYQ services. Should WBC divert, the tight utilisation of the wide-body aircraft would probably mean that a cancellation SYD-MEL would have to be made to restore the balance. The lateness of NBP on-line would not be considered a problem, as it would probably only amount to a minor delay. At this stage, continued liaison with Crewing, CJM, Engineering and, of course, the Port Coordinator would best prepare the IOC, and no further action can be taken as yet.

UPDATE @ 1150 EST

SYD Port Coordinator advises the following update.

a) NBO has landed.
b) WBC has now been given additional holding of 10 minutes, resulting in the crew electing to divert to MEL immediately due to low fuel reserves (ETA MEL 1255).
c) As the conditions at the airport continue to improve, NBR, WBB, WBE and WBA are all expected to land according to their current estimated holding times.

With the airport now slowly returning to normal, and since NBO has landed, the thought now is to balance the loss of WBC in SYD. Either WBC has to refuel and return to SYD (if the ETA MEL is 1255, the best re-departure is about 1340 with an ETA into SYD of 1505). But

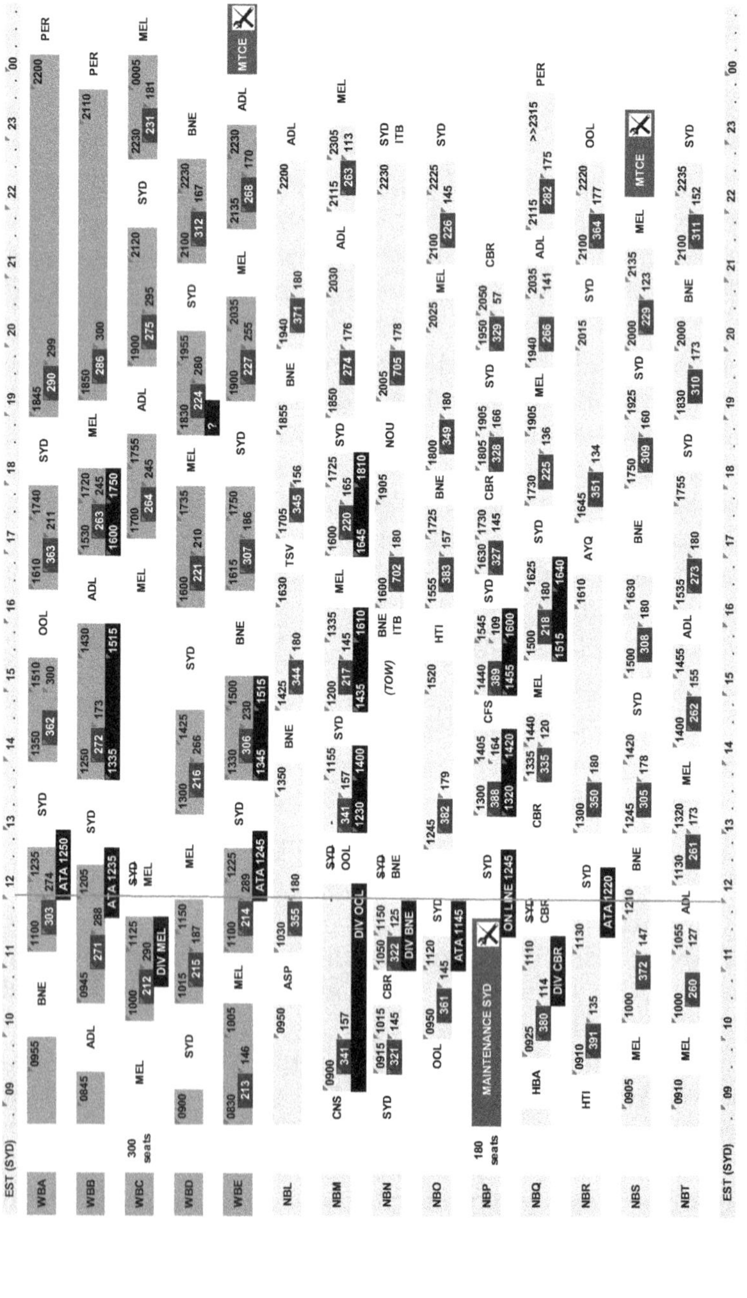

WEATHER SCENARIO: *THUNDERSTORMS AT SYD*

Figure 7.5 SYD weather – solution

WEATHER SCENARIO: *THUNDERSTORMS AT SYD*

the subsequent delays to any of the flights (and therefore patterns) out of SYD with extensive delays all evening, would suggest that removing some more flying now will be less disruptive overall.

The IOC, therefore, will instigate the following changes:

a) Cancel 219 SYD-MEL. (The CJM team will consider ways to accommodate all 213 customers who will fit across a number of flights (e.g., 35 seats on 217 – delayed, 90 seats on 221, 46 seats on 225 and 45 seats on 227).
b) Then it is a matter of swapping around the patterns of the wide-body aircraft. Normally, the optimum solution would be for the first available aircraft to be used to recover the disruption. In this case, WBB is the first aircraft expected into SYD and this aircraft is selected to operate 272 SYD-ADL (this aircraft will achieve the least delay), 263 ADL-MEL (a conservative delay is set at this time in case delay time improves), and then rather than delaying 224 MEL-SYD, a change with WBD can be made in MEL, so WBB operates 286 MEL-PER.
c) WBA will operate 362 SYD-OOL, 363 OOL-SYD, 290 SYD-PER. (Liaison with Maintenance Watch will confirm whether WBA can operate to PER overnight (i.e., there are no maintenance limitations preventing this.) WBB was always planned to overnight PER so there is no base change for this aircraft.
d) WBC on return to MEL, remains on the ground to operate 264 MEL-ADL.

These changes are shown in Figure 7.5 opposite.

FINAL UPDATE

The remainder of the aircraft land in SYD and effectively this disruption has concluded. All aircraft issues have been managed, three cancellations have been implemented, and four diversions have occurred. The disruption to customers is, of course, regrettable, but the IOC is responsible for the running of the network in its entirety, and to sustain network schedule integrity some sacrifices become necessary. In summary, the disruptions have not been excessive in this scenario.

MULTI-ENGINEERING SCENARIO

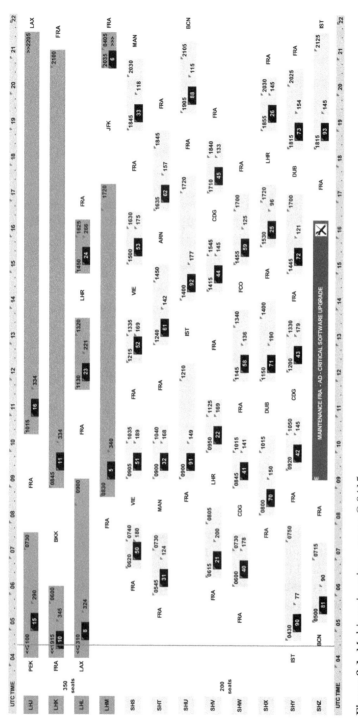

Figure 8.1 Multi-engineering – status @ 0415

- All times in the scenario relate to UTC time.
- A timeline indicates the current time in the scenario.
- Prior to the timeline, all flights are operating on schedule.
- Flight numbers are shown on dark background.
- Actual booked loadings are shown to the right of the flight numbers.
- Flights exceeding timescale are shown with << or >>
- For this scenario, DUB, LHR and MAN are UTC time, ARN, BCN, CDG, FCO, and FRA are UTC + 1 hr, IST is UTC + 3 hrs, BKK is UTC + 7 hrs, PEK is UTC + 8 hrs, JFK is UTC − 5 hrs, and LAX is UTC − 8 hrs.
- The utilisation is not intended to simulate any existing airlines. It is only a representation.

8

MULTI-ENGINEERING SCENARIO: *UNSERVICEABILITIES IN THE NETWORK*

BRIEF

The airline has an international operation based in FRA. The fleet consists of four twin-engine, wide-body, long-haul aircraft (registrations/tails designated LHJ-LHM) and eight twin-engine, narrow-body (single-aisle) aircraft (registrations designated SHS-SHZ). The capacity of the wide-body aircraft is 350 seats and the narrow-body aircraft 200 seats. Minimum turnaround time between passenger flights for wide-body aircraft is 90 minutes and for narrow-body aircraft is 60 minutes.

SCENARIO DESCRIPTION

Refer to Figure 8.1 opposite.

The time is 0415. Maintenance Watch have just completed compiling the Maintenance Status Report which provides the engineering status for all aircraft and maintenance equipment within the network for the day, and are delivering it to the Operations Controllers handling both European and long-range international networks.

MULTI-ENGINEERING SCENARIO

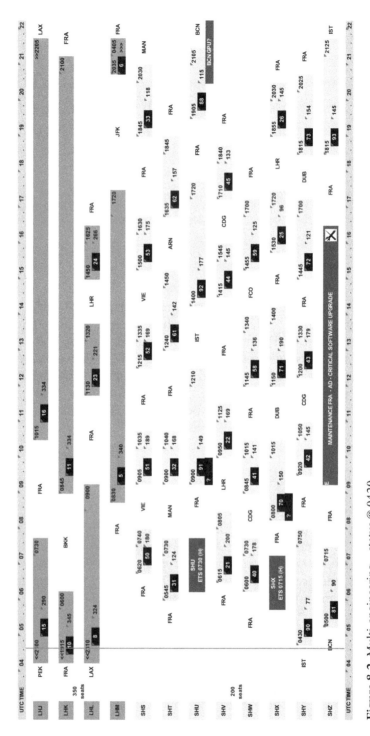

Figure 8.2 Multi-engineering – status @ 0420

MULTI-ENGINEERING SCENARIO

IOC INTERACTION

The Maintenance Status Report covers the following:

a) SHU in FRA has been undergoing a windscreen change overnight, but the sealant initially failed to adhere correctly which has delayed the curing time. The current ETS is 0730 at the hangar.

b) SHX in FRA has a flap disagreement problem. Engineers are currently re-rigging flaps and expect an ETS of 0715 at the hangar.

c) SHZ is scheduled for maintenance (0900–1600) in FRA. This is a compulsory software upgrade (aircraft is under an AD from the manufacturer).

d) The GPU in BCN is currently U/S, awaiting parts from FRA to fix it. The airline has borrowed a GPU from a local airline to use for SHZ's departure at 0500 if required. Engineers have checked the status of SHZ's APU and don't expect any problem with the engine start-up and departure.

e) They request SHU in FRA tonight in position for the Work Package 6A – Cabin Configuration modifications tomorrow.

The Engineering report is updated on the Gantt chart according to Figure 8.2 opposite.

With four early morning flights from FRA (SHS, SHT, SHV and SHW) forming a large part of the first wave of departures, the IOC will be relieved that none of these has a maintenance issue. The GPU problem in BCN won't affect Flight 81 SHZ departing at 0500, and no flights are scheduled into BCN until later, so no further thought is warranted at present, but a note made to check the status of the GPU later in the day. Similarly, the request to position an aircraft overnight is not high priority this early, especially with ongoing maintenance issues. Thus, the attention of the IOC is drawn to the unserviceable aircraft, which, with a reasonably tight utilisation, may have detrimental effects on immediate and later flights should the problems not be rectified. Both of these engineering problems may be straightforward, but both can also develop into more lengthy problems. The Controller may well quiz Maintenance Watch further as to their own gut feelings regarding the confidence in both ETSs. Experienced Engineers comprising the Maintenance team in the IOC are no different to experienced Controllers. Their sense of knowing exactly what key information to extract and from whom is a prized skill, as is an ability to 'read between the lines', to interpret communications appropriately and then make an informed judgement call.

The first question the IOC raises is to establish whether there is another aircraft that can cover one or both of the unserviceabilities. The Gantt chart reveals the following. SHY 90 IST-FRA arrives at 0750 with a ground time of 90 minutes before operating 42 to CDG. Notably, SHZ arrives 0715 and is not committed for flying, but rather to undergo maintenance. So the Controller has a number of questions for Engineering. First, would be for the Controller to pursue with Engineering the use of SHZ to cover the morning operations. Second, is to get a sense of how confident Maintenance Watch are in relation to both of the unserviceable aircraft. If one were favoured over the other in terms of meeting its ETS, that aircraft might be preferred to operate the first of the two departures (Flights 70 and 91).

UPDATE @ 0515 EST

Maintenance Watch have confirmed with the Engineering Director that SHZ is definitely not available for flying commitments due to the AD requirement. Further, Maintenance are confident that SHX will be serviceable by 0700 and on-line at 0745. They are less assured regarding SHU as the windscreen sealant is a new product which has not been used before. They believe the ETS of SHU is more likely to be about 0815 at the hangar.

The latest information from Maintenance Watch confirms that SHZ cannot be part of any solution, at least for the present. IOC would have scanned the loadings across the fleet to establish if any flights can be cancelled. However, the Gantt chart reveals that most flights are heavily loaded. SHX on-line at 0745 will likely only incur a small delay on 70 FRA-DUB, and it is the first aircraft available to operate that flight. With less confidence in the ETS of SHU, the IOC has to consider the best way to commit that aircraft. Here, the options would include swapping patterns around such that the U/S aircraft is committed to a later departure if this is possible. Sometimes, the seemingly obvious change may not be the best, as certain flights, routes, or patterns may need to be given preference for commercial or operational needs. The important thing is that the number of options are thoroughly explored and assessed. Even with the limitations in the current utilisation, there are still opportunities to mitigate the maintenance issue.

MULTI-ENGINEERING SCENARIO

Taking these circumstances into consideration, the IOC can instigate the following changes:

a) Retain SHX on 70 FRA-DUB. The rationale is that there appears to be quite a low probability that the aircraft will be delayed further, and provided 0745 is a firm time on-line, the combination of paperwork finalisation, towing (from the hangar to the gate) and then the crew pre-flight checks should only amount to a minor delay on 70 FRA-DUB, and given the aircraft has a lengthy turnaround time in DUB, it is most likely that delays will be contained to one or perhaps two flights only. Should the ETS drop back, longer delays on 70/71 may have to be accepted.

b) With an ETS on SHU of 0815 at the hangar, the aircraft could be expected on-line at about 0845. The action would therefore be to swap SHU and SHY in FRA once SHY arrives at 0750 (i.e., swap the patterns for the remainder of the day). This gains 20 minutes to cover SHU's later ETS while protecting the longer 91/92 FRA-IST-FRA service in favour of 42/43 FRA-CDG-FRA. Should times drop back at all, there would be no option other than to delay 42/43 accordingly.

These changes are shown in Figure 8.3 overleaf.

UPDATE @ 0520 EST

The IOC (Maintenance Watch) has just received an ECAM (electronic centralised aircraft monitor) message from LHK operating Flight 10 en route FRA-BKK. The aircraft is close to the top of descent into BKK, but the crew have also been alerted (also via the ECAM system) to a hydraulic problem – the aircraft is losing pressure in the *Green System* hydraulics. Maintenance Watch have alerted Ops Control. Meanwhile, they have begun to interrogate the ECAM system through the aircraft's ACARS facility. A conference call has been set up between the IOC, Maintenance Watch and the operating crew of LHK.

The immediate thought processes are for the safety of the aircraft, taking into account the remainder of the flight, and in particular whether the landing in BKK will be normal or abnormal. First, the IOC needs to

MULTI-ENGINEERING SCENARIO

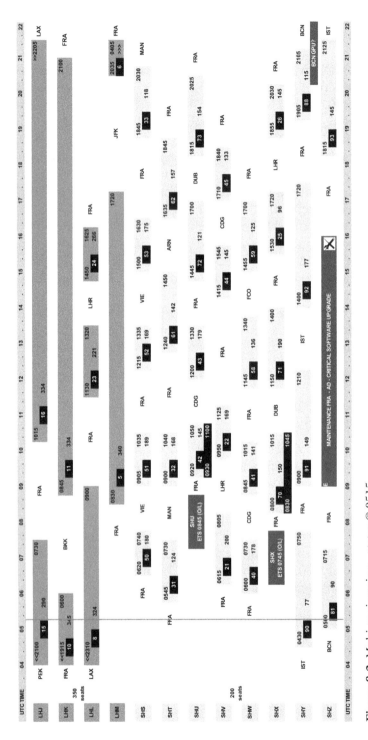

Figure 8.3 Multi-engineering – status @ 0515

MULTI-ENGINEERING SCENARIO

establish from Maintenance Watch the exact nature of this unserviceability. (If the crew deem the landing to be abnormal or an emergency, more responses need to be undertaken by the IOC.) As it stands, forewarning Social Media in the IOC may be judicious, even at this early stage. The conference call between the IOC, Maintenance Watch and the operating crew will ascertain the circumstances of the problem, and any resulting safety and/or operational irregularities, so the attention in the IOC can then turn to the next commitment of the aircraft. The Gantt chart shows that the turnaround time on the ground is just under three hours and there is no other aircraft in the vicinity that could become part of a solution. The next commitment for the aircraft is Flight 11 scheduled to depart BKK at 0845, and which is virtually full. Those customers will begin checking in shortly. Also needing to be clarified are the crew arrangements regarding Flight 11.

The information sought by the IOC includes the following in relation to Engineering:

a) What does this hydraulic problem mean in the context of this flight? Is it likely to cause any problem in-flight or in relation to landing?
b) What aircraft systems may be affected by the loss of *Green System* Hydraulics?
c) Will the aircraft be U/S on arrival BKK? If so, for how long?
d) What is the likelihood of parts being needed? Where from?
e) Are there suitably qualified Engineers (and sufficient manpower) available to inspect and fix the aircraft?

The following is sought in relation to both Crewing sections:

a) What is the sign-on time for the crews in BKK and what is the maximum ToD (this establishes how much delay or other disruption can be tolerated)?
b) If the problem resulted in delaying Flight 11, can the crews be held at the hotel (i.e., deferring sign-on time to prevent duty hours being used)?

MULTI-ENGINEERING SCENARIO

And the following in relation to the BKK Airport Manager:

a) What is the weather expected at arrival time? (If rain or strong winds are expected, the crew may elect to divert to an airport with calmer conditions.)
b) Is there any media presence either there or expected? (The rationale would be to prepare for any commentary or questioning that might arise in case the media learn of an 'aircraft incident'.)
c) Should the aircraft become disabled on the runway after landing (due to the loss of hydraulic systems), does ATC need to be notified of the possible loss of a runway for some time?

If there were a simple fix to the problem such as a physical replacement line or fitting or some adjustment in relation to the ECAM system, there would be no need for any IOC action, with the expectation that the aircraft could be made serviceable within the current scheduled ground time. However, if this were to develop into a hydraulic pump change and/or other changes of significant components, a delay is more than likely on Flight 11. Major considerations now relate to the crew duties and for the curfew in FRA. The STA of Flight 11 is 2100 UTC, which is 2200 local FRA time, and with the curfew beginning at 2300, there is only a one-hour grace period.

UPDATE @ 0530 EST

Maintenance Watch have interrogated the aircraft's ECAM system and also referred to the various maintenance databases. It appears that there is no previous history of hydraulic problems with LHK. The ECAM system appears to be normal with no erroneous readings apparent. They have also just finished speaking with their contracted Lead Engineer in BKK. The advice is that if it's a hydraulic pump change, parts will be needed and that the fix could be lengthy. In that case, the aircraft probably won't make departure time. They also confirm that the *Green System* supplies hydraulics to the nosewheel steering so although the landing is expected to be normal, there may not be nosewheel steering available for taxiing (this means the aircraft will have to shut down all engines on the runway and be towed to the gate). The Engineers cautioned that they won't know anything more until the aircraft lands and they have a chance to examine further. The ETA is 0604.

MULTI-ENGINEERING SCENARIO

With this information the IOC have a lot to consider:

a) The crew duty time is not the overriding problem should the aircraft not meet departure time. The problem becomes arriving before curfew in FRA.

b) Can the work be conducted on the line (i.e., at the gate), or must the aircraft be towed to a hangar? (This would be a considerably longer and more extensive process.)

c) Should the Engineers expect the problem to be resolved within a few hours of arrival, the crew should sign on at the normal time (0715 – 90 minutes prior to departure).

d) However, should the aircraft be delayed more than one hour, the curfew will prevent the flight departing BKK (based on scheduled block time). If that's the case, then there's little point bringing the crew out to the airport. The curfew in FRA operates from 2300–0500, so if the flight failed to operate on the current day, it would need to be rescheduled to arrive FRA immediately after curfew ends (i.e., 0500 arrival). In that case, Flight 11 would depart BKK at 1645, requiring the crew to sign on at 1515, so one option would be to hold the crew at the hotel until later.

e) If such a delay were to occur, can a new slot be negotiated for the FRA arrival time?

f) If the crew were to come to the airport and sign on, and *then* the aircraft's serviceability deteriorated, the crew would have to take another full rest break (e.g., 12 or so hours once signed off), thereby delaying the flight even further. So, the sooner the engineering estimates are made, the sooner all the other factors start to fall into place.

g) The next thought relates to the customers checking in at BKK. The IOC would need to consult with the Station Manager to establish if they wished to show any delay on the flight yet (to the public), both on the departure boards and by direct contact with customers via electronic media.

h) The CJM would need to check with their accommodation provider(s) should the aircraft not be able to depart during the day. This would also include transport and meal vouchers.

MULTI-ENGINEERING SCENARIO

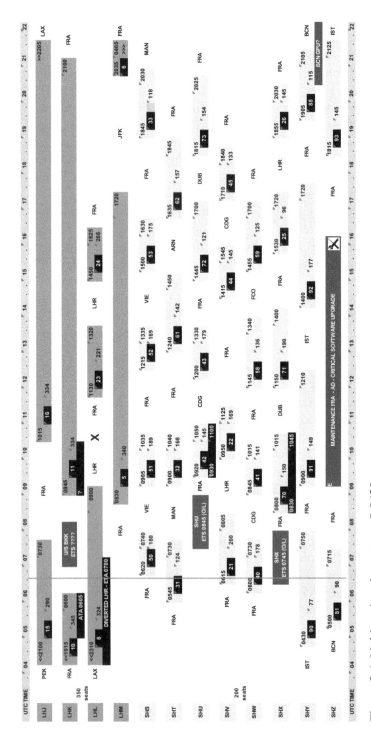

Figure 8.4 Multi-engineering – status @ 0620

UPDATE @ 0610 EST

The Airport Station Manager advises that LHK has landed safely. No emergency was declared and, consequently, no fire trucks or other vehicles attended. However, as expected, the aircraft did not have any nosewheel steering, so is currently disabled on the runway. Right now, a tug is approaching the aircraft to tow it into the bay. Once on stand, the Engineers will begin to look at it.

UPDATE @ 0620 EST

In the IOC, the Duty Controller has received a SATCOM call from the crew of Flight 8 LHL en route LAX-FRA. The flight crew on this aircraft is a 'heavy crew' consisting of a Captain, Senior First Officer and two Second Officers. The First Officer has called to advise that the Captain has had a medical event during the flight and has been rendered incapacitated. Accordingly, he has been moved to the crew rest facility for the remainder of the flight. As a result, the First Officer is remaining in the left seat in the cockpit, and has taken command of the flight (i.e., has assumed the role of *Pilot in Command*). As they are currently flying over UK airspace and with 150 minutes still to be flown to FRA, he has decided to divert the aircraft into LHR, and accordingly notified ATC by calling a PAN-PAN alert and also requested a priority landing. ATC have advised that the ETA of the aircraft into LHR is 0700. These changes are shown in Figure 8.4 opposite.

The diversion into LHR is the highest priority. With a diminished technical crew, the safety and operation of the aircraft is of paramount importance. So, the IOC will need to know what arrangements are being made on the ground in LHR for the landing and then what medical assistance will be organised to assist the Captain. Crewing will take care of this aspect, but the IOC Duty Manager will need full awareness of all arrangements being undertaken. Again, social media input in the IOC will be invaluable due to the unscheduled diversion, no matter what customers on board may be informed by the Operating Pilots and Senior Cabin Crew. Similarly, there would be considerable company communication to be disseminated not only to fleet management but senior company management as well.

Although LHR is an operating port for the airline, it is not a crewing base for either type of aircraft operated. Thus, the thought is for rescuing the aircraft by ascertaining the first available (wide-body licensed)

MULTI-ENGINEERING SCENARIO

crew to bring the aircraft on to FRA as soon as possible. The aircraft has 324 customers, and the IOC doesn't want it stuck in LHR. Clearly, the Captain can't continue, but the question would be asked of both Crewing functions – can the rest of the crew continue within duty time if another Captain were available to bring the aircraft on? Primarily, is there another Captain in LHR? If not, where would the nearest Captain be? If there was none close by at all, the nearest is likely to be in FRA. However, finding then dead-heading a Captain from FRA will take quite a while and could not be achieved in time for the other crew members to continue duty, so a complete crew (Technical and Flight Attendant) would be required. Clearly, this would delay the continuation of Flight 8 considerably more.

 Crewing advise that there is a Captain in LHR who has been undergoing simulator training in LHR and who is rostered to dead-head this afternoon on Flight 24 (LHL) at 1450. She is legal to fly (e.g., has duty time available and has not consumed alcohol for at least eight hours), and, because Flight 8 has a heavy crew, she can join the existing complement provided the three original technical crew do not exceed their ToD limitations. Crewing have contacted her and expect her to sign on at 1000. Both Pilot and Cabin Crewing sections have by now spoken with their respective inbound crews, and confirm that all crew members can continue to FRA.

With the relief Captain signing on at 1000 in LHR, the aircraft, once on the ground, can be pre-loaded, fuelled and otherwise be ready to go, just requiring the new Captain's final approval. So, the IOC can work on a 1030 departure from LHR. The Controllers then have to reconcile the rest of the aircraft's pattern for the day. The continuation of the flight would arrive FRA at 1205, but the aircraft is currently committed for Flights 23/24 FRA-LHR-FRA (using LHL). There is no other wide-body aircraft available in FRA at the same time, but a scan of the Gantt chart reveals some narrow-body aircraft availability. The loadings on both of these flights exceed the capacity of the narrow-body aircraft type, but staying with LHL would mean delaying a total of 487 customers about two hours, whereas a number of narrow-body aircraft could actually be used (by swapping patterns around) to operate 23/24 on time. In consultation with Crewing, Commercial (CJM), and the Duty Station Managers at both FRA and LHR, a plan to interchange wide-body and narrow-body aircraft can be proposed, such that all flights operate on or very close to schedule.

MULTI-ENGINEERING SCENARIO

The plan to resolve the delays could be as follows:

a) Flights 23/24 FRA-LHR-FRA are *downgraded* to a narrow-body aircraft. The overbookings (over the 200 seats on the narrow-body aircraft) would be accommodated on 25/26 (see (b) below).
b) Flights 25/26 FRA-LHR-FRA are *upgraded* to a wide-body aircraft (using LHL).
c) Several narrow-body patterns are *swapped* to utilise the ground times. Basically, by using the first aircraft in to operate the first flight out around the 1130–1240 times, all flights can operate to schedule.
d) The only downside is that the overbooked customers on Flight 23 (21 customers) now travel on Flight 25, four hours late, and 66 customers originally booked on Flight 24 now travel on Flight 26, four hours late.

The changes to incorporate this appear as Figure 8.5 overleaf.

However, the plan is incomplete. At the bottom of Figure 8.5, are two flights unallocated to any aircraft. These are Flights 44/45 FRA-CDG-FRA. Notably, customers would be completely oblivious to this detail. Customers booked on 44/45 would still be expecting to fly as per their booking as no indication of any other arrangement will have been made or advised to them. Leaving the aircraft unallocated is an internal airline situation and the IOC members and other stakeholders (e.g., airport staff) will be fully aware that further changes need to occur at some point. In addition, no gate would necessarily be known at this stage either. There are a number of options for these flights as shown below:

a) SHX arrives FRA at 1400 and could operate 44/45 delayed about 45 minutes each flight.
b) By swapping patterns again, SHU could operate 44/45 delayed about 15 minutes each and SHX could operate 72/73 (with a small delay on 72 only, due to the long turnaround time in DUB).
c) Maintenance could be monitored throughout the day to establish if SHZ (undergoing the AD) is likely to be available for flying earlier than expected. This may be possible perhaps by increasing manpower on the work to be performed, or ascertaining if any of the work can be deferred until that night or another appropriate time. If SHZ were to operate 44/45, the aircraft could be positioned overnight in FRA for that work (by using any of SHS, SHW or SHY to operate 93 to IST). The point is that there are options, and the IOC is bound to explore any possible ways to maintain schedule integrity.

MULTI-ENGINEERING SCENARIO

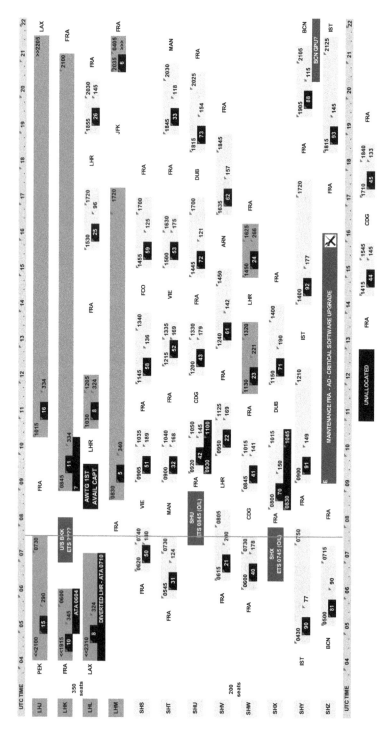

Figure 8.5 Multi-engineering – solution

MULTI-ENGINEERING SCENARIO

d) In any event, a delay would not be set on 44/45, either for this reason or in the likelihood that later disruptions may make delaying these now, pointless.

The key elements of the scenario are then really complete. The plan for LHK either becoming serviceable for a departure within an hour of schedule or having to operate later has been conceived, so the situation becomes a 'wait and see'. The adjustments for SHU and SHX have also been determined. Other than a significant change in any of these, the flights would operate largely as shown in Figure 8.5 opposite.

9
OPERATIONS CONTROL
IN THE FUTURE

INTRODUCTION

Like all domains with opportunities to embrace technological processes that can surpass human effort and brainpower, problem solving in the IOC is increasingly becoming the focus of high-tech organisations. The ability of humans to remain in-the-loop is still critical but more and more, airlines are using complex solution software to assist the management of disruptions. This chapter considers the key drivers likely to affect ways in which IOCs function in the future. In particular, new challenges in the industry, innovative advances in technology, increasing needs and demands *of* humans and demands *on* humans, and a need to respond correctly and with due alacrity to a range of external influences will govern the future make-up and roles of tomorrow's IOC.

INDUSTRY

Industry challenges will continue to test the resolve of the best IOCs. Parallels with the irresistible force meeting the immovable object are evident. Sheer growth of passenger and freight movements, expansion and development of airports, and requirements for more efficient infrastructure and supporting services are driving the momentum of the travel experience. Containing this powerful energy are nullifiers such as severe congestion, escalating pollution, wariness or even rejection of travel based on social or environmental opinion, and general dissatisfaction with suboptimal performance in the face of continual disruption. These pressures both *on* industry and caused *by* industry alike will continue to compel airlines to recognise and address shortfalls in customer delivery. Thus, IOCs will need to acknowledge the foreseeable conflicts and arm themselves with the right tools and people.

TECHNOLOGY

Aviation is arguably one of the most technology-dependent industries ever. Continuous improvement in airframe and propulsion technology drives the very nature of the travel business, but on the ground and at the heart of operating an airline network at any airport, in any region across the world, lies an enormous bank of sophisticated systems. Improvements in current and emerging systems drive the operational future. Every single aspect of airline operations revolves around technical capability, for example, from improved satellite-based navigation and landing performance, aircraft systems of maintenance for monitoring, interrogation and assessment of in-flight operations, to communications systems that rapidly link flight deck decisions with customer outcomes. On the ground, advanced technologies that enhance airport equipment and facilitation must realise significant benefits (e.g., lower landing minima, better ATC flow), under increasingly challenging weather and trying traffic conditions – i.e., gains in efficiencies need to outweigh current limitations. Accessing more advanced global databases will enable better weather predictability and provide avoidance mechanisms of phenomena such as volcanic or cyclonic activity. And in the IOC, more complete and capable systems need to provide intelligent information, filtered for preciseness and relevance, but inclusive of key data that properly inform and drive decision-making processes.

STAFF

The future IOC needs to be populated with highly capable individuals. Past recruitment methods may have worked to a degree, but future performance is critically dependent on strategies to source and secure the right blend of characteristics and skills. Doubtless, some change is needed. Finding, training and retaining those individuals who can absorb and, importantly, visualise the 'big picture', think 'outside the box', and who have a naturally inquisitive but relentless mindset that drives passion, should be the key focus. Merely filling a vacancy should have no place in future IOCs. Now, more than ever, high-performing individuals must be the basis of engagement, so recruitment and selection processes need to be far more directed at determining what constitutes the right person for the task and then set about acquiring that resource. No longer can an IOC afford to entertain a candidate who at first appears to meet criteria, but when tested, fails to deliver in the short term, and probably will in the longer term. Training needs must also be fulfilled, not just to cover the fundamentals of the job, but advanced techniques need to deliver well-honed skills in problem recognition, analysis and solving. Recurrent training should be part of that strategy, so as to engage and revitalise the employee contract and with it develop individual growth and maturity of thinking.

EXTERNAL INFLUENCES

Previous disruption-management strategies have had a significant impact on customer reactions. Airline disruptions that deteriorate into extensive ground-holding times now need quite specific management. In past events, customers have remained on board aircraft for long periods of time, to the extent of significant detrimental health and well-being effects. This action may have been taken by the airline to contain disrupted passengers, or with the knowledge that circumstances would change imminently to enable a resumption of operations. However, in the interests of consumer protection, legislation in many jurisdictions now prohibits such treatment of customers. The legal (and financial) ramifications for an airline failing to meet the new requirements are now far greater than just adverse social media commentary that prevailed earlier. Accordingly, the philosophy in the IOC has changed as well. For example, decisions affecting specific operations may force airlines to consider customer management on board active flights, and thereby react far earlier to events such as, for example, severe pending or existing weather conditions.

SOCIAL MEDIA

The growing influence of social media is now requiring airlines to have social media teams embedded in the IOC, with the appropriate support to monitor and respond to a variety of social media platforms and network chat sites. Policy changes are required due to the ability for a customer on board an aircraft, and therefore currently en route to a destination, to produce and broadcast a message that may well reach a diverse range of social media followers on the ground. In the past, information about an incident occurring on an aircraft was largely reliant on journalists checking with an airline media team prior to the event reaching either the newspapers or the nightly news. Nowadays the information is instantaneous. A message is likely to include video and sound and, in many cases, its intended audience has received it on their own devices before the airline is even aware of it being circulated. Indeed, the customer now has just about as much information on his/her portable device as has the Operations Centre. They know where their inbound aircraft is, they know what the destination weather is going to be, they can look up the runway in use, and they can get their connecting information – all at 40,000 ft. In addition, they can promptly receive their delay or cancellation advice directly from the IOC at the same time as the airline's own sources.

FINAL COMMENT

This text has tried to convey some of the information and processes about airline IOCs. More can always be said, and additional scenarios can be so diverse that they could number in the hundreds, but the risk of repetition makes for a fairly ordinary reception. So, the intention in Part II of the text was to highlight some typically representative problems faced by airlines and provide sufficient detail so as to explain to the reader the complexities of the task at hand in an IOC. The authors trust that the message has been illustrated meaningfully.

NOTE FROM THE AUTHORS

If you are lucky enough to be working in an IOC or are considering it, you'll find it frustrating, stressful and at times exceptionally difficult. The decisions made will impact hundreds and at times thousands of customers, both internal and external. On busy days you will leave work absolutely drained. But, it is unique, enormously rewarding and actually makes a difference. It is totally different to any other department within an airline.

BIBLIOGRAPHY

Abdi, M.R. & Sharma, S. 2007. Strategic/tactical information management of flight operations in abnormal conditions through Network Control Centre. *International Journal of Information Management*, *27*, 119–138.

Bazargan, M. 2010. *Airline Operations and Scheduling*, Farnham, Ashgate.

Bruce, P.J. 2011. *Understanding Decision-making Processes in Airline Operations Control*, Farnham, Ashgate.

Bruce, P.J., Gao, Y. and King, J.M.C. (eds) 2018. *Airline Operations: A practical guide*, Abingdon, Routledge.

FAR FC. 2018. *Federal Aviation Regulations for Flight Crew. Rules for Air Carriers, Operators for Compensation or Hire, and Practical Ownership Programs.* US Department of Transportation. Aviation Supplies and Academics Inc. Newcastle, Washington.

IATA Worldwide Slot Guidelines. 2017. 8th Edition English version. Retrieved 01/10/19 from www.iata.org/policy/slots/Documents/wsg-8-english.pdf

Van Vliet, V. 2012. Henry Gantt. Retrieved 17/09/19 from ToolsHero: www.toolshero.com/toolsheroes/henry-Gantt/

Wu, C.-L. 2010. *Airline Operations and Delay Management*, Farnham, Ashgate.

INDEX

ACARS 77, 85, 91, 179

Aircraft Planner 41–42

alternates 32, 41, 70, 105, 107, 109–110, 113, 118–119, 147–148, 150, 153–154, 160–161, 163, 167

AOG 117–118

ATC: clearance 60, 64, 108, 112, 147, 161, 171; communication with 93, 106–107, 123, 143–144, 163, 169, 171, 182, 185; delays 118–119, 134; holding 105, 112, 150, 152, 160, 165; industrial 126; issues 96; negotiating with 40; requirements 39, 55, 92, 109, 111; rules and procedures 39, 109–110; services 60, 63, 131, 161; traffic flow 17, 45, 93, 192

authority *see* decision making

autonomy *see* decision making

awareness *see* decision making

back-up IOC 13, 95

buffers *see* utilisation – buffers in

cancelled/cancellations 59, 73, 94, 96, 98, 102–103, 108, 114, 118, 126, 128, 130, 132, 134, 140, 143–144, 155–157, 165–166, 168–169, 172–173, 178

CDL xvii, 39, 63, 70, 95

charter flights 5, 49, 64, 67, 70–71, 74, 98, 126, 160

Chicago Convention 4

complexity *see* decision making

connecting passengers/connectors *see* tranships

crisis 6, 21

crew connections 57–58, 88, 90

crew duty (hours/times/limitations) 4, 43, 59, 62, 88, 100, 102, 110, 120–121, 140, 152, 157, 181, 183, 186

dead-head (position or 'pax') 90, 121, 155, 186

decision making xxii, 8, 10, 13–14, 23, 27, 29, 37–38, 44, 50, 93, 135, 169, 192; arbitrator 20; authority 4–5, 14, 18, 20, 48, 76, 98, 142; autonomy 14, 48, 76, 132; awareness xxii, 13, 22, 26, 31–32, 40–41, 46, 76, 79, 82, 93, 96, 98–99, 129–130, 185; complexity 3, 16, 26, 30, 82; rationale 3, 5, 60, 122, 179, 182

decision making styles 33; intuitive 30–31, 33, 40, 99; proactive 12, 42, 96, 99, 103; rational 29, 34, 40; reactive 8, 14, 31

delayed/delays 60, 68, 73, 85–86, 94, 96–98, 100, 102, 104, 107–108, 110–111, 113–114, 118–119, 125, 128, 134, 140, 142–144, 153, 155, 157, 163, 173, 179, 183, 187; absorption 86, 160; causation 125–126; effects 130; extent 111, 113, 128, 132, 163, 173, 179; minimising 102, 108, 169, 179; potential 97–98; reporting of 102; resolving 187; rolling 118; subsequent 124, 173

disabled aircraft 119–120, 182, 185

diverted/diversions 64, 73, 92, 94, 99–100, 102, 105, 107, 111–112, 117, 119, 132, 134, 150, 152–153, 155, 157, 163, 165–167, 169, 173, 184, 188

ferry (flights/ferrying of aircraft) 98, 101–103, 155, 160, 166–167

first wave 96, 98, 177

flight blocks (puks) 78–82, 85–86, 91–92, 97, 158

gaps *see* utilisation – gaps in

ground stop program 118

INDEX

IATA xiii, 60
ICAO xiii, 4

low cost carriers 8, 52

maintenance: check 111; costs 66; equipment 41, 63, 95, 175; facilities 9, 170; function 42; icon 86, 88; in IOC 177; information 86; intervention 41; issues 85, 98, 100, 115–117, 177–178; limitations 173; procedures 64, 68; release hours 170; requirements 42, 56, 95; schedule 69, 97, 100; service 86; status 41, 95, 175, 177; support 73; work 56, 58, 63, 70, 73, 86, 92, 97, 103–104, 170
MEL xix, 63, 70, 95, 116

non-revenue *see* ferry

on-time performance (OTP) 94, 102, 133–134
OOOI xiv
operational control xxi–xxii, 4–5, 13, 25; defined 4
Operations Control Centre i, xxi, 3–5; as centre of excellence 10; hierarchy 17–18; metrics 6, 9, 94, 134; nerve centre xxi, 5; systems and tools xxi–xxii, 5, 7–9, 17, 21, 23, 25, 33, 35, 37–38, 76, 79, 94, 133, 192; technology 9, 11, 23, 191
Operations Controllers: disposition of xxi, 18, 27; downtime 28, 99; experience 23–25, 29–37, 99, 130, 135, 154, 177; expertise i, xxi, 6, 14, 16–17, 20, 26, 30, 33, 34, 76, 93, 101, 154; fatigue 27, 99; leadership 20, 28, 33, 38; motivation 26, 29; novice 30; outstanding 26; recruitment xxi, 7, 21, 24, 33, 35, 193; selection xxi, 21, 33, 35, 193; self-management 27; situation awareness xxii; (initial situation awareness) 31, 96, 154; (full situation awareness)

31, 88, 185; sixth sense 22; skills 22, 24, 26, 28–29, 31–32, 34–36, 40, 43, 193; thought processes i, xxii, 29, 34–36, 104, 128, 130, 135, 136, 153, 165–167, 171, 177, 179, 183, 185; training xxi, 7, 21–23, 29, 33, 36–38, 50, 193

policy 10, 13, 18, 72, 76, 98, 106, 194
problem-solving xxii, 4, 17, 22–24, 26, 31, 37–38, 43, 50, 135, 191
productivity 9, 21, 52
puks *see* flight blocks

Routers 17

slots 45, 60

tranships (connections) 61, 86, 88–89, 104, 128, 140, 142, 150, 165
turnaround (turn) times 46, 58–59, 61, 86, 97, 100, 133, 147, 159, 175, 179, 181, 187

utilisation: buffers in 57, 86, 111; gaps in 86, 97; robustness 57, 72

volcanic ash 41, 72, 94–95, 103, 128, 192

weather: blizzard 9, 98; cloud 104, 106, 108–109, 111, 160; fog 41, 74, 88, 98, 104–108; icing conditions & treatment 41, 63, 94, 104, 111, 113–114; snow 104, 113; temperature effects 61, 66, 73, 98–99, 104, 114–115; thunderstorms 41, 74, 94, 98–99, 104, 108, 111–113, 160, 166; typhoon/cyclone/hurricane 9, 71, 94, 103–104, 111, 115; wind 107, 109–112, 129, 165; (crosswind) 63, 110; (headwind) 92, 102, 109; (tailwind) 92, 109; windshear 61, 110, 165
what-if scenarios 26, 92, 99, 150